14 Days
W9-AYP-555
OCT 21 '67
DEC 2 '67
MAR 13 '68
APR 18 '69
NOV. 20 1987
NOV 08 1994
WITHDRAWN

THE
INFAMOUS WALL
OF BERLIN

THE INFAMOUS WALL OF BERLIN

Why was it built?
Will it ever come down?

A Study of Its Political
and Military Implications

by Monro MacCloskey
Brig. Gen. USAF (ret.)

The Berlin Wall has come to be a symbol far transcending its mortar and brick. It stands as a reminder to free people everywhere of the dangers of Communism—that in a world where anyone is shackled, no one is truly free. This informative history gives a vivid picture of the Wall from its beginning.

About the Author

Brigadier General Monro MacCloskey, USAF (Ret.), a command and jet pilot, began his career in 1920 as a West Point cadet. Not long after the outbreak of World War II, he was ordered to England as a member of the staff charged with organizing the 12th Air Force and planning the invasion of North Africa. He participated in the first assault landing in North Africa, and later became Deputy to the Assistant Chief of Staff for Operations of the 12th Air Force, with headquarters in Algiers.

In the course of the war, General MacCloskey held a wide variety of posts, including those as Chief of Organization, Training, and Equipping Section, Operations Division, Northwest African Air Force; a member of the Joint Planning Staff of the Mediterranean Air Command; and Assistant Director of Plans for the Mediterranean Allied Air Force. He

(Continued on back flap)

ALSO BY MONRO MAC CLOSKEY

Your Future in the Air Force
How to Qualify for the Service Academies
Reserve Officers Training Corps
You and the Draft
NATO
Secret Air Missions
Pacts for Peace

The Infamous Wall of Berlin

MONRO MacCLOSKEY
BRIGADIER GENERAL, USAF (RET.)

RICHARDS ROSEN PRESS, INC., NEW YORK 10010

Library of Congress Catalog Card Number: 67-10037

Published in 1967 by Richards Rosen Press, Inc.
29 East 21st. Street, New York City, N.Y. 10010

First Edition

Manufactured in the United States of America

DEDICATION

This book is dedicated to the courageous and freedom-loving Germans living on both sides of the Infamous Wall of Berlin.

Preface

. . . We must and shall continue to act in concert with our allies in the common effort toward achieving a just and enduring peace for ourselves and for Europe. We must and we shall continue to contribute our full share toward the security efforts of the West. But at the same time we must contribute our own judgments and our own initiative toward creating a happier relationship between our state and the states around us, both friendly and unfriendly.

Let me be specific. We want to bring some movement into what is known as the German problem. Not movement for the sake of movement, to give only the appearance of progress. There is an interdependence between the division of Germany and the split of Europe. Therefore we want to see movement with direction and purpose, movement that will bring us closer to a solution of the postwar dilemma that continues to keep Europe divided.

Our people will not be satisfied with a divided Germany in a divided Europe. Their respect for justice, for the right of self-determination, for freedom, is now too well developed. Their coming of age has been powerfully influenced by the principles of Western democracy. It is not reasonable, and it is not wise, to expect them to put these principles on a shelf and wait for others always to act for them.

The German people are well aware that they alone cannot bring about the reunification of their country. They have no illusions on this score. They know that until the Soviet Union is prepared to accept the reunification of Germany, the country will remain divided. And they know that it would be foolhardy for the Germans alone to attempt to negotiate with the Russians without prior understanding with the allies. The peace settlement is a community undertaking in which Washington, London, and Paris, as well as Bonn, must be equally involved if not equally active. . . .

WILLY BRANDT, MAYOR OF WEST BERLIN

(Extract from an address in New York City on April 19, 1965.)

About the Author

Brigadier General Monro MacCloskey, USAF (Ret.), a command and jet pilot, began his career in 1920 as a West Point Cadet, graduating in 1924. Shortly after the outbreak of World War II, he was ordered to England as a member of the staff charged with organizing the 12th Air Force and planning the invasion of North Africa. He participated in the first assault landing in North Africa, and later became Deputy to the Assistant Chief of Staff for Operations of the 12th Air Force, with headquarters in Algiers.

In the course of the war, General MacCloskey held a wide variety of posts, including those as Chief of Organization, Training and Equipping Section, Operations Division, Northwest African Air Force; a member of the Joint Planning Staff of the Mediterranean Air Command; and Assistant Director of Plans for the Mediterranean Allied Air Force. He organized, equipped, trained, and commanded the 885th Bomb Squadron (H) Special of the 15th Air Force, which engaged in the night dropping of intelligence and resistance personnel and supplies into Southern France, Northern Italy and the Balkans, and the 15th (later redesignated the 2641st) Special Group, which performed similar functions throughout Europe. In addition, General MacCloskey flew fifty combat missions.

After the war, General MacCloskey attended the National War College and upon graduation was appointed Chief of the Air Intelligence Policy Division at AF Headquarters. He served as Air Attaché to France, Belgium and Luxembourg, and at the time of his retirement was the Commander of the 28th Air Division, Air Defense Command.

His World War II decorations include the Silver Star; Legion of Merit with Cluster; Distinguished Flying Cross; Air Medal with seven Clusters; EAME (Europe-Africa-Middle East) Medal with nine Stars and one Arrowhead; Army Commendation Medal with Cluster; two French Croix de Guerre with Palm and two with Gold Star; two

French Legion of Honor, one Degree of Officer and one Degree of Commander; Order of the Partisan Star; and Decoration of the Sultan of Morocco.

General MacCloskey has also written *Your Future in the Air Force, How to Qualify for the Service Academies, Reserve Officers Training Corps, You and the Draft, Secret Air Missions, NATO, Guardian of Peace and Security,* and *Pacts for Peace,* all published by the Richards Rosen Press, and *The United States Air Force, Its Roles and Missions,* published by Frederick A. Praeger, Inc.

Contents

Charts and Illustrations

Foreword

The division of Germany, and with it the division of Berlin which was the capital of the German Reich until 1945, has given rise to one of the foremost controversies of the century. Volumes have been written on the history and culture of Germany, the Nazi era of World War II, the occupation of Germany by Allied forces and the nation's postwar political, social and economic development. The focal point of the German problem, however, is Berlin.

It had been laid down in the three-powers "London Protocol" of September 12, 1944, that Greater Berlin, as a special area outside the Zones of Occupation, was to be occupied jointly by the armed forces of the United States, the United Kingdom and the Soviet Union. French participation was provided for in a supplementary protocol.

Totally different interpretations are held by the United States and its Western Allies and by Russia on the German question and its settlement. It is here that the two most powerful nations in the world confront each other in a hostile atmosphere. No such confrontation of nations has ever required more delicate handling and sober thinking than the present perilous impasse.

As a result, fundamental interests of the world powers have become extremely involved in Berlin affairs since World War II. Commitments made by the Western democracies have been rigidly maintained and respected. The future of Berlin, however, lies in a solution of the global conflict between the forces of Communism and those of the Free World. Berlin has been used as a testing ground of the strength and purposes of the Soviet Union and nations of the free world. It is conceivable that this issue might one day touch off World War III.

Berlin has weathered many crises since 1945: the Soviet blockade in 1948; the Soviet threat to turn over the Russian Sector in Berlin to the East German government and withdraw its troops from Germany—accompanied by the demand that the Allies do likewise (1958); and the building of the Communist wall in 1961. Berlin has been and still is the scene of an East-West power struggle that includes not only a reunification of Berlin but a peace settlement with Germany.

This book is designed to describe the political and military background of the Berlin Wall and its implications. It traces the important events related to the Berlin problem from the London Protocol of September 1944 to the present. It deals with the roots of the Berlin issues, the four-power control of the city, the Allied airlift, the dividing wall, conditions in East Berlin, Soviet aims in Berlin, and the free world's stake in the controversy.

As this book is being written, a further complication has arisen in an already complex situation—France has announced its intention to withdraw her troops from NATO, and possibly from West Germany and Berlin. In June, 1966, the final communiqué of the NATO Foreign Ministers Meeting stated that the Supreme Military Headquarters would be withdrawn from Paris and relocated in Belgium and that NATO military commands would be consolidated and streamlined. However, it also stated that the fifteen partners agreed the Atlantic Alliance "is as necessary today as ever." Its primary aim continues to be the "common defense of all member countries."

President de Gaulle's separatism cannot but have a significant effect on inter-Allied as well as international relations, but speculations as to the eventual outcome lie in the field of journalism, due to the day to day developments.

Much of the material in this book has been obtained from government historical records, U.S. Department of State sources, and from the files of the German government. Special thanks are due the Press Counselor of the German Embassy in Washington and representatives of the German Information Center in New York for their generous co-operation.

MONRO MACCLOSKEY
BRIGADIER GENERAL, USAF (RET.)

WASHINGTON, D.C.
JUNE, 1966

THE
INFAMOUS WALL
OF BERLIN

(German Information Office)

The Infamous Wall of Berlin, Potsdamer Platz

Chapter I

German History in Brief

In the recent past, Germany has lost two world wars during which eight and one-half million Germans perished. Twice within twenty-five years the value of its national wealth expressed in money and securities has had to be written down to less than 10 per cent of its original value. Now, the eastern boundaries of the Federal Republic of Germany are the same as those of the free western world. Because the zonal boundary forms the dividing line between the East and the West, Germany is today the center of world-wide political, diplomatic, and military interest and concern.

Germany is a country that has been prominent in world affairs since the beginnings of European history. Its position as a nation without natural borders in the middle of Europe has made it a corridor of violent migrations of peoples through the centuries. Furthermore, religious schism divided the German people and paralyzed the country for several generations. Such circumstances have, over the centuries, affected the physical size of Germany and its political decisions.

The Holy Roman Empire

After the great migration of nations, the Teutonic branch of the Indo-European family of languages broke up and yielded, among others, the German tribes. These consisted of the (Lower) Saxons and Frisians in the north, the Franks in the west, the Thuringians in central Germany, the Alemanni in Swabia, and the Bavarians in the south. They were united under one of the greatest figures of the early Middle Ages—Charlemagne (Charles the Great).

Charlemagne codified the laws, founded many schools throughout Europe and on Christmas Day, A.D. 800, was crowned Charles I, Emperor of the Holy Roman Empire, by Pope Leo III. Charlemagne was devoted to the principles of Christian religion. He revered the

Church of St. Peter the Apostle in Rome above all other sacred places. After his death (814), he was made a saint. His son, Louis I, was crowned Emperor of the Holy Roman Empire at Aachen, Germany, in 814. He founded the Carolingian dynasty.

Louis II, Charlemagne's grandson, king of all Germany east of the Rhine River by the Treaty of Verdun (843), and his descendants were unable to hold the realm bequeathed to them. In 987, Louis V, King of France and the last of the German Carolingian family of rulers in France, died. By that time, scores of dukedoms had become virtually independent.

Otto I, who became a German king in 936, was crowned Emperor of the Holy Roman Empire in 962. He and his successors engaged in many wars in a vain effort to resurrect in the Middle Ages the ancient Roman Empire under German rule. With the death of the last of the Hohenstaufen dynasty, a German princely family which ruled Germany in 1138-1208 and 1215-1254, no central government remained to enforce law and order. For many years, the German princes struggled for the crown, but, meanwhile, the power of the territorial princes steadily increased.

After 1520, the Reformation was the most momentous event of early German history. Since the sixteenth century, Germany had experienced a religious schism which the Thirty Years' War (1618-1648) was not able to overcome. It began in 1517 when a German priest, Martin Luther, became involved in a series of public religious differences with the Catholic church. Following these disputes, Luther was formally excommunicated by the Pope in 1521. The effect was to divide Germany in a series of European wars, primarily between the Protestants and Catholics of the Holy Roman Empire.

During this period, the title of Holy Roman Emperor of the German nation had passed to the Hapsburg dynasty, a German princely family in Austria, which cherished the illusion that some day it might re-establish the former Roman Empire. The Treaty of Westphalia ending the Thirty Years' War, while crushing Austria's hopes, also divided Germany. The Netherlands, which had been alienated from the First Reich since 1556 through the domination of the Spanish Hapsburgs, and Switzerland finally relinquished their association with the Reich. Until its dissolution in 1806, the Holy Roman Empire was known as the First Reich.

The 18th century witnessed the growth of Brandenburg-Prussia to a great power and a spiritual, artistic, and intellectual golden age exemplified by such individuals as Johann Sebastian Bach, the great composer; Immanuel Kant, the noted philosopher; Johan Wolfgang Goethe, poet, dramatist, novelist, and philosopher; and Friedrich Schiller, poet, dramatist and writer. It was also the age of Frederick the Great, one of the most famous kings of Prussia (1740-1786), who defeated a great coalition of nations—France, Austria, Russia, Poland, Sweden and Saxony—and won Silesia.

The Holy Roman Empire of the German nation, which had assumed more and more the character of a federation of states, collapsed in 1806 under the onslaught of the French Emperor Napoleon. In 1815, the Deutscher Bund was formed as a loose association of thirty-two princes and free imperial cities. It was succeeded in 1867 by the Norddeutscher Bund, the immediate predecessor of the German Reich of 1871. Its emperor was the King of Prussia. Austria, which had provided German emperors for 600 years, ceased to be a part of Germany in 1866.

The German Empire

The new German Empire, or Second Reich, the first chancellor of which was Otto von Bismarck, led the German people from 1871 to 1914 to great economic prosperity, especially in the field of industrial production. The living standards of the people reached noteworthy heights. In 1881, Germany was the first nation to introduce model social legislation. Scientific, technical, and cultural achievements brought high praise for the Reich from around the world. Germany's part in starting World War I and its subsequent actions in the prosecution of the war brought shock and disillusionment to many.

The German Republic

German unity, however, remained preserved when, after losing World War I (1914-1918), the Reich became a republic, even though there was a considerable loss of territory under the terms of the peace. The Emperor Kaiser Wilhelm II abdicated, and a democratic system was established with the Weimar Constitution of August 11, 1919. In accordance with the United States' President Woodrow Wilson's "Fourteen Points" and the wishes of the victorious powers, it was intended that there should be a rearrangement of European territory after 1918 on the basis of the right of the peoples' self-determination. In the peace treaties, however, the principle was not followed. In the east, a plebiscite was arranged in only small parts of the territories placed under the alien administration of the victors. In each plebiscite, the population elected to remain within the German Reich.

Danzig and Memelland, whose inhabitants also wished to remain within the German union, were given international status. Yet, in spite of this, Memelland was illegally annexed by a Lithuanian *coup d'état* in 1923.

From the time of its creation the Weimar Republic was handicapped by reparations and inflation, as well as by difficulties in the field of foreign politics. Its internal weakness was reflected in the frequent changes of government. Eventually, there were thirty-six parties vying with each other for the favor of the electorate. Germany, dependent on exports and foreign credits, was particularly hard hit by the world economic crisis of the thirties. From 1930, the parties of the extreme right and extreme left increased rapidly, so that the center parties supporting the state were no longer able to form a parliamentary majority.

The Third Reich

It was this situation that made it possible for Adolph Hitler to become head of the strongest party. As such, he was nominated Chancellor of the Reich in 1933. Through his own and his associates' unscrupulousness, together with the pressure of the masses behind him, he succeeded in eliminating every one of the constitutional organs and transforming the Republic into a formless despotism. The policies pursued by the National Socialists under Hitler unleashed World War II in 1939, which ended in Europe in May, 1945, with the total military defeat of Germany.

In June, 1945, under the provisions of the Potsdam Agreement be-between the three Allied powers, the territory of the Reich was partitioned into four Zones of Occupation, with the Berlin area under four-power status. The eastern provinces were placed under either Polish or Soviet Russian administration pending a final peace settlement. In the west, the Saar territory, with a German-speaking population of 1,000,000 inhabitants, was attached economically to France under a system of partial political autonomy. In 1956, the Saar government was recast according to the will of its population as the result of a free election and a friendly agreement reached between France and Germany. On January 1, 1957, the Saar became a part of the Federal Republic.

The Federal Republic of Germany

It was not until 1949 that the provinces and states of West Germany formed the German Federal Republic. The German Reich has not ceased to exist as State and Subject in international law because of its unconditional surrender in 1945. Rather, it has been temporarily deprived of its competence to perform legal acts as a result of the abolition of its central organs. With the merging of the three Western Zones of Occupation in 1949, the Basic Law (Constitution) was adopted to give a new order to political life for a transitional period until the German State organs were once more competent to perform legal acts. The Basic Law, therefore, reorganized the German state that had not ceased to exist in 1945, with the Federal Republic of Germany carrying on the German Reich under a new name. For this reason, the Republic considers itself as a trustee of the German state that has existed since 1871, until reunification takes place. More than 54 million Germans live in the Federal Republic and an additional 2.2 million in West Berlin, compared with 18 million in other parts of the Reich. Only the Federal Republic has a democratic, freely elected government. Only this government can, therefore, act and negotiate on behalf of Germany as a whole. These circumstances have led to the fact that the Federal Republic, as the legitimate continuation of the German Reich during the transitional period, is frequently called Germany in other countries.

In October, 1943, the Moscow Conference of Foreign Ministers of the Allied Powers established a European Advisory Commission which deliberated until November, 1944, on the partition of Germany into occupation zones. In a protocol dated September 12, 1944, the Commission stated that the border between the Western zones and the Soviet zone should follow the administrative borders within Germany, viz., the western borders of Mecklenburg, Saxony-Annhalt, Thuringia, and the northern border of Bavaria. On June 16, 1945, in a telegram exchange between United States President Truman and Soviet Marshal Stalin, it was agreed that the Soviet forces should advance on July 1, 1945, to the Soviet zonal border as it is today.

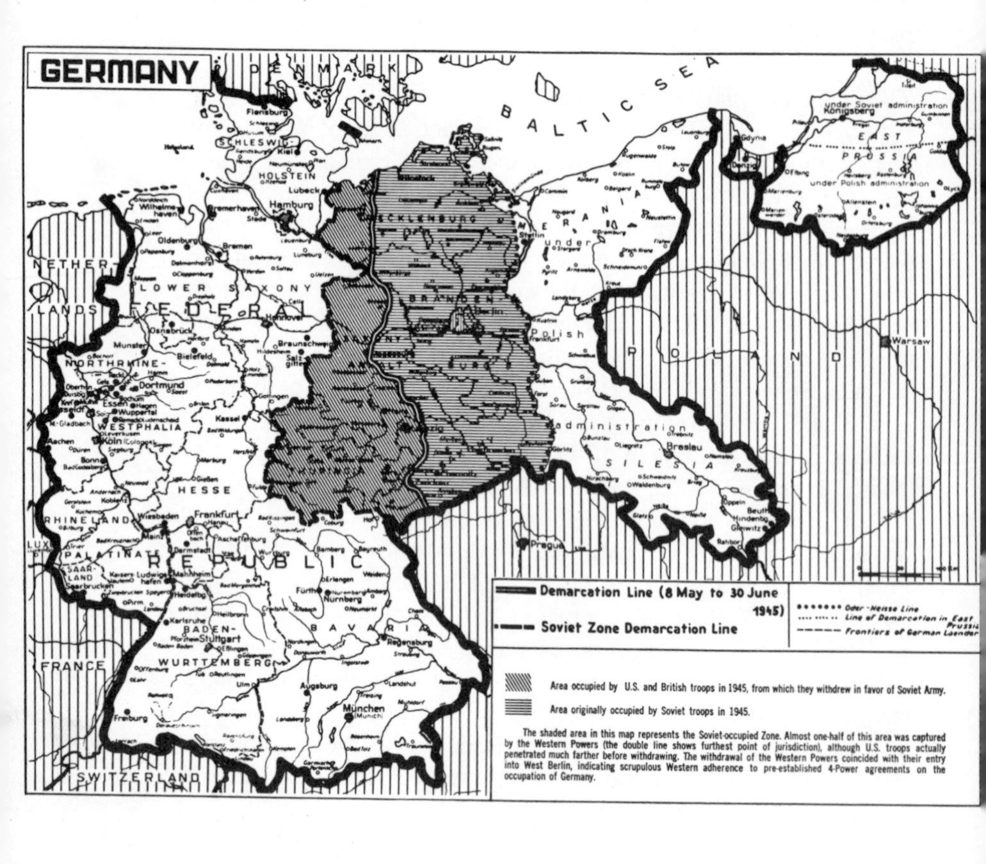

The shaded area in this map represents the Soviet-occupied Zone. Almost one-half of this area was captured by the Western Powers (the double line shows furthest point of jurisdiction), although U.S. troops actually penetrated much farther before withdrawing. The withdrawal of the Western Powers coincided with their entry into West Berlin, indicating scrupulous Western adherence to pre-established 4-Power agreements on the occupation of Germany.

The Zones of Occupation administered by the Allied powers and later relinquished gave the USSR Saxony, Saxony-Annhalt, Thuringia, and Mecklenburg, and the former Prussian provinces of Saxony and Brandenburg. The territory east of the Oder-Neisse line within the 1937 German boundaries comprising the provinces of Silesia, Pomerania, West Prussia, and the southern part of East Prussia, totaling about 41,220 square miles with a population of 9.6 million (1939), is under Polish administration. Northern East Prussia is under Soviet domination. The United States has not recognized these changes or the East German regime. The state of war with Germany was ended by the Western Allies in 1951 and by the USSR in 1955. The area of Greater Berlin is described in the following section.

When the December, 1947, quadripartite Council of Foreign Ministers failed to reach agreement on the establishment of German central administrative agencies, the three Western Powers and the Benelux (Belgium, Netherlands and Luxembourg) countries concluded the London Agreements in June, 1948, in which they resolved to let the Western German people establish their own government on the basis of a democratic provisional consititution. In August, 1948, the legislature of the eleven *laender* (states) in the French, British, and American zones chose sixty-five delegates to a "Parliamentary Council" charged with the drafting of such a provisional constitution. The "Basic Law for the Federal Republic of Germany" was adopted by the Council on May 8, 1948, and was subsequently approved, with some reservations, by the three Military Governors.

The Federal Republic of Germany was proclaimed May 23, 1949, effective September 1, 1949, in Bonn, the new seat of government. The occupying powers, the United States, Britain, and France, restored German civil status on September 21, 1949. On May 5, 1955, the occupation statute was terminated and the Federal Republic of Germany became a sovereign state with full authority in its internal and external affairs.

The Parliament consists of two chambers: the Bundestag, the lower house, which has 499 voting members from the Republic and 22 nonvoting observers from West Berlin; and the Bundesrat, the upper house, which represents the states. It has 41 delegates from the *laender* and four nonvoting members from West Berlin. The Bundesrat president serves one year and acts as deputy to the federal president.

The federal president, who represents the Republic internationally, is elected by a specially convened Federal Convention which consists of the members of the Bundestag and an equal number of members elected by the legislatures of the constituent states. Elected for a four-year term and eligible for a second consecutive term, he is the highest official in the Republic and has representative rather than executive functions. He normally proposes and, upon request of the Bundestag, appoints or dismisses federal ministers, judges, and public servants, and promulgates federal laws.

It is the federal chancellor who determines, and assumes responsibility for, general policy. He is elected by a majority of the Bundestag upon proposal by the federal president. He nominates the federal ministers, who are in turn formally approved by the federal president. Ministers conduct their business on their own responsibility within the limits of the chancellor's general policy. The Bundestag may express its lack of confidence in the chancellor only by electing a successor by a majority vote and by requesting the federal president to dismiss the chancellor. Thus, the chancellor's position is more secure than that of a prime minister in most other European countries where a simple vote of lack of confidence or a defeat on a major piece of legislation can topple the government.

West Germany is a member of the North Atlantic Treaty Organization, the European Coal and Steel Community, the Common Market, and the Council of Europe. It also belongs to the International Monetary Fund, the United Nations Educational, Scientific, and Cultural Organization (UNESCO), and the European Community of Atomic Energy.

The German Federal Republic has experienced tremendous economic growth since 1950. The gross national product rose from $23.1 billion in 1950 to $94.2 billion in 1963. Its index of industrial production increased from 100 in 1958 to 144 in 1963. West Germany leads Western Europe in steel production. Germany lost most of its merchant marine during World War II, but since then the industry has rebuilt rapidly and had exceeded its pre-war merchant fleet tonnage by January 1, 1964. The economic recovery of West Germany since 1945 is due in large part not only to its own strenuous efforts but also to the tremendous amount of financial aid given it by the United States.

Berlin

It was rather late in Germanic history when the city of Berlin emerged. In 1701, it became the capital of the state of Brandenburg-Prussia. In 1871, after the defeat of France by Germany, Bismarck, the Prussian chancellor, formed the German Empire and was proclaimed King Wilhelm I of Prussia, German Emperor, in Versailles on January 18th. Berlin was made the capital of all the German Reich. By the early nineteen hundreds, Berlin had also become the center of German art, culture, intellectual life, and the drama. Prior to World War II, Berlin had a population of 4,338,800 and was one of the largest cities in the world. It was the greatest industrial city of Germany, specializing in the manufacture of machine tools, electrotechnical equipment, food and beverages, and clothing. It was the center of a railway system from which seventeen lines branched out to all parts of the country. It also contained many famous educational institutions, music academies, and national museums.

In the summer of 1945, the great city lay as if dead. Its center was an area of vast debris. Some 26 per cent of its homes and dwellings and 53 per cent of its apartments had been destroyed or heavily damaged. The population had dropped to about 3,000,000. Many monumental landmarks had vanished forever, except for the Reichstag, the Parliament building housing the elective legislative assembly, which is being restored.

Berlin today is a city of unbelievable contrasts. West Berlin is very impressive with its new handsome and magnificent buildings, its sparkling elegance and pulsating spirit, and with comparatively few relics of World War II remaining. It is in sharp contrast with the drabness and poverty of East Berlin. *Unter den Linden* was a gay, bustling boulevard and the main street in pre-World War II days. Now it is entirely within the Soviet Sector of Berlin and bears no resemblance to its former self. In West Berlin it has been replaced by *Kurfurstendamm,* where the shops, restaurants, and places of entertainment are throbbing with life and activity. Stores are stocked full of goods and crowded with buyers, and tourist offices are jammed with travelers. West Berlin's economy is obviously at a high level.

The mood of the West Berliners has changed greatly since the early post-war years. Where they once feared that the Soviets could stir up a crisis at any time, they now are confident that it will not happen. The withdrawal of a battalion of U.S. troops from West Berlin provoked no protest. There are still 6,000 American troops on duty and, as the West Berliners see it, that is enough. West Berlin has an area of 186 square miles and a population of 2,189,000 (1961) as compared with 156 square miles and a population of 1,055,000 in East Berlin.

Berlin is a sprawling metropolis which lies 100 miles behind the Iron Curtain within the Soviet-occupied zone of Germany. It is not, however, part of that zone. It is a separate political entity for which the four major Allies of the war against Nazi tyranny are jointly responsible. Its special status stems from the fact that it was the capital not only of Hitler's Third Reich, but of the German nation formed in the latter half of the nineteenth century. In essence, the four major Allies agreed to hold Berlin, as the traditional capital, in trust for a democratic and united Germany.

Chapter II

Roots of the Berlin Problem

The roots of the Berlin problem are long and tangled, going all the way back to the crucial year of 1944 when the three Allied powers were making agreements on the zones of occupation in Germany and the administration of Greater Berlin. By the close of the war, while the military coalition between the Soviet Union and the Western Allies was still in force, these agreements were concluded.

The initial Allied (United States, United Kingdom, and Soviet Union) occupation plans for Berlin as well as for Germany had been prepared in London by the European Advisory Commission. These plans were subsequently reaffirmed on several occasions by the Allied powers. Under the agreement, Berlin was to be divided for occupation purposes into four sectors. East Berlin was to be under Russian control while West Berlin was to be allocated to the United States, United Kingdom, and France. The entire city of Berlin was excluded from the four zones into which Germany was divided. Each of these zones was to come under one of the four Allied powers, and Greater Berlin would fall within the zone under Russian occupational control. The Allied Protocol on the zones of occupation in Germany and the administration of Greater Berlin is contained in Appendix I. Excerpts from the Allied Agreement on Control are in Appendix II.

Although the occupational status of Berlin had been agreed upon in September, 1944, the military task of capturing the city was left to the Soviet Union. Great Britain and the United States concentrated their military efforts on defeating the German forces with the object of ending the war as quickly as possible. Thus, when the German forces were conquered, the United States and Great Britain were in fact occupying far more of Germany than had been laid down in the September, 1944, agreement.

Since this agreement was acknowledged as binding on the three signatory nations, the American and British forces relinquished to the

Russians a territory amounting to almost half the area of the Eastern Zone and half its population. Had the Western Allies been fighting the war with purely military calculations, they would probably have fought for and taken Berlin before the Russian forces. However, the Western Allies were primarily concerned with winning the war as part of the coalition that included the Russians and they regarded the military problem as one to be solved by the coalition acting as a unit. Consequently, military considerations were made to conform to the legal agreements between the three powers.

Until the arrival of the Western military governments in Berlin in July, 1945, Soviet authorities had been in sole charge for ten weeks. During this time they had systematically removed and shipped to Russia most of the machinery and equipment that could still be used, including machines and tools from the larger manufacturing plants, generators from power stations, buses, street-cars, underground trains, and 52 automatic telephone exchanges with a 250,000-line capacity. Eighty-five per cent of all the city's industrial installations which had not been destroyed in the bombing were seized by Soviet unilateral dismantling operations, together with about 70 per cent of its stocks of raw and finished materials. Soviet looting added to the heavy damage inflicted on Berlin during the war and immensely increased the difficulties of restoring order and sustaining life in the Western sectors of the city.

Politically, the Soviet military administration took advantage of the capture of Berlin by immediately establishing a new city government under an appointed Magistrat, the executive organ of the city government, which was largely controlled by Moscow-trained German communists and by infiltrating Soviet agents in the police force. Unfortunately, the actions taken by the Soviet military administration and the communist-dominated Magistrat were approved by the three West Berlin Commandants upon their arrival in Berlin. This decision established the status quo of Berlin and was prescribed on July 11, 1945, in the first quadripartite order issued by the Allied Kommandatura, the Allied governing body for Berlin described in Chapter IV. At the time the full implications of the order were not realized. Later, however, the Kommandatura and the Western-minded city leaders devoted considerable effort to canceling this hasty action. This proved extremely difficult because of the Soviet veto in the multipartite conferences.

Despite the establishment of the provisional city government, the Western Allies insisted on the right of the people of Berlin to elect their own government. To forestall the threat to them from a free election, the Soviet authorities attempted to force a merger of their Communist Party with the traditional German (noncommunist) Social Democratic Party. In their Eastern Zone of Occupation, the Soviets were able by heavy pressure to merge the two parties into the so-called Socialist Unity Party. But in Berlin, where they were compelled to share control with the Western Allies who in turn could guarantee the people freedom of choice, they lost.

In accordance with the Kommandatura letter of August 13, 1946 (Appendix III), the first and only all-Berlin election in which residents of both East and West Berlin voted was held on October 20, 1946. The results were as follows:

Social-Democratic Party	48.7 per cent
Christian Democratic Party	22.2 "
Socialist Unity Party (communist)	19.8 "
Liberal Democratic Party	9.3 "

In a city with a long history of radical politics, and where the Soviets were in a commanding position, it was remarkable that the communists won less than a fifth of the votes and only a fifth of the seats in the city Parliament. From the Soviet point of view, the results of the election were disastrous, particularly since many districts of Berlin had been communist for decades, and the many communists appointed to key posts by the Soviets could presumably have been relied on to deliver large numbers of votes.

The Berliners responded with unmistakable clarity, probably because they were reacting to Soviet pressures, or perhaps due to the memory of Soviet occupation practices during the first ten weeks the Russian armies were in sole control of Berlin, and to the conduct of the Red armies throughout Germany. In reprisal, the Soviets awaited an opportunity to divide the city which had dared to elect a Parliament with an anticommunist majority. On June 24, 1947, the Parliament of Greater Berlin chose Professor Ernst Reuter, a Social Democrat, as mayor; whereupon the Soviet authorities split the Senate of Greater Berlin by refusing to acknowledge Reuter's election. On August 12, 1947, Reuter was rejected by the Allied Commandants on a Soviet veto. As a result, Louise Schröder served as acting Mayor, the first woman in Prussian history to hold that office.

It had become apparent that the Soviet government, unable to have its own way under democratic procedures, was not going to collaborate in the joint operation of the occupation regime. On March 20, 1948, the Soviet High Commander, Marshal Sokolovsky, left the Allied Control Council meeting, thereby terminating the operation of the Council as a joint administration. This arbitrary behavior by a senior representative of the USSR was evident in many aspects of the city administration. It was most obvious in the police force which was under control of the Kommandatura but in which the Soviet agents in the police force took their instructions only from Soviet officials. Eventually the city government achieved control over the police in the Western Sectors of Berlin, but in the Soviet Sector the communist police officials remained in power and continued to receive their orders from Soviet authorities.

In the Soviet Zone of Germany, the Russians acted promptly to tighten their control over the area. They refrained from implementing the provisions of the Potsdam Agreement directed at the reconstruction of German political life on a democratic basis. The Potsdam Agreement resulted from a conference (July 17-August 2) between United States President Truman, Soviet Premier Stalin, and Great Britain's Prime Minister Winston Churchill, who was replaced by Prime Minister Attlee on July 25th.

The Soviets enveloped the emerging administration of their zone with totalitarian communist control at all levels, filling key positions with veteran German communists, many of whom had spent the war years in the USSR. The most famous of these was Walter Ulbricht who was later to become chairman of East Germany's highest governing body. He had been trained in Moscow's Lenin Institute during 1926-1929 and returned to the Soviet Union in 1937 or '38 where he remained throughout World War II. Ulbricht became a Soviet citizen and came back to Germany in 1945 as a colonel in the Soviet Army.

Soviet officials systematically eliminated all political opposition to communist authority in the Soviet Zone. This process was accomplished mainly by the "single ticket" whereby the communists were allotted a majority of seats before an election had taken place. At the same time, a number of supposedly independent satellite parties were permitted to exist under communist control. This was the same procedure that was employed in Poland, Rumania, Hungary, and Bulgaria, and it violated the democratic pledges made by Premier Stalin in the Yalta declaration on Poland and on liberated Europe.

Other provisions of the Potsdam Agreements affecting the German economy were also ignored or opposed by the Soviets. Germany was neither treated as an economic unit nor allowed to reconstruct and support itself. In December, 1945, the Soviet authorities vetoed a proposal to open zonal borders to allow Germans to travel back and forth. They also failed to comply with the principles of pooling manufacturing facilities of the Soviet Zone with those of the Western Zones. Meanwhile, they continued the removal of industrial equipment and machinery from the Soviet Zone and refused to account to the Western powers for anything removed. Furthermore, most of the agricultural yield of the Soviet Zone was commandeered by the puppet Soviet Zone authorities and shipped to Russia.

This high-handed method of administration by Soviet government officials led to the organization of two political communities in Germany. In Western Germany, the basic right of self-determination was not only sanctioned but actively encouraged. The entire political structure of West Germany was completely reorganized and the foundation of democratic life was firmly established on all levels, beginning with free local elections and rising to state elections. In Western Germany there were no obstacles hindering communist political activity. Nevertheless, the communist party was so ineffective that it failed to secure even the 5 per cent of the popular vote needed to enter the parliamentary race in the second elections to the Bundestag in 1953.

Because of the cross-purposes of the Soviets and the Western Allies, the German economy was still in a chaotic condition for almost a year after V-E (Victory in Europe) Day. The United States, with Great Britain's concurrence, made another effort to treat Germany as one economic unit by proposing the establishment of central German administration agencies, free trade between the zones, and a concerted program of balanced imports and exports.

By late 1946, it had become clear that the Soviets were acting in accordance with their long-range plans for communist domination of the world. Their short-range goals were to establish outright communist regimes in eastern and central Europe wherever the Red armies had invaded and occupied during and after the war, and to increase communist control over other regimes in southern and western Europe.

In the fall of the same year, the British and American Occupation Zones were merged for economic purposes into one unit. A short time later the French Zone joined in the new economic unit.

In December, 1947, following the fifth session of the Council of Foreign Ministers of the four Occupation powers, the Western delegates jointly concluded that no agreement with the Soviet authorities in Germany could be reached except "under conditions that would not only enslave the German people but would seriously retard the recovery of all Europe."

The Western two-thirds of Germany, ultimately to become the Federal Republic of Germany, consisted of the three Western Zones of Occupation containing about fifty-three million inhabitants under a democratic, freely elected regime in which political and economic life could proceed within the framework of democratically controlled free enterprise. The same democratic way of life was established in the three Western Sectors of Berlin with its 2,189,000 citizens.

The Soviet Zone of Germany with 17 million inhabitants, and East Berlin with a population of 1,055,000, were under the control of a regime maintained by secret police, guns, and tanks. Since the end of the war, it has been administered by the characteristic Soviet Communist Party supported by a subservient police system.

Thus, two irreconcilable political regimes were set up on German soil as a result of the break-up of the military coalition that had conquered Hitler.

Chapter III

Berlin's Cold War

In this generation, the decisive factor in international politics is the Cold War—a state of affairs in which the free world is committed to resist communist aggression, expansion and subversion. The Cold War began almost the moment World War II ended on the ruins of the military coalition that had won it.

One unfortunate heritage of World War II is the division of Germany into two diametrically opposed political communities. The western two-thirds of German territory exercised its right of free choice and became politically integrated into the Western bloc led by the United States. The remaining German territory was forced into the Soviet orbit with central Germany organized into a communist satellite and the easternmost part of the country put under Russian and Polish administration. This bifurcation of Germany reflects the division of Europe and the world into Eastern and Western blocs and not only creates sharp friction in the heart of Europe but is also a constant source of irritation in world politics.

The division of Germany is brought into sharper focus by the partitioning of Berlin. The city is identified with the principles of German statehood and the German people cannot give up the concept of Berlin as the capital without relinquishing their hopes for national reunification. Berlin entirely in communist hands would put German unification under the symbol of communist hammer-and-sickle. Furthermore, the struggle for Berlin includes not only the legitimate aspirations of Germany but also the cause of world freedom itself.

Berlin is a key factor in the flux of contemporary politics. Through divided existence it emphasizes the split between two great world powers. Since it is in the heart of Germany, it represents a political goal of paramount importance to both the East and the West. To achieve this goal, the communist-controlled Soviet regimes in East Germany and East Berlin have created three major Berlin crises since 1945 that will be described in subsequent chapters. Each time the Soviet government has exploited the division of Berlin as a tactical expedient to apply pressure on the free world in accordance with Soviet worldwide strategy.

It was the decision of the Soviet Union to withdraw from the Allied coalition and embark on its program of world domination that initiated the Cold War and split Germany in two. This eliminated any possibility for the joint administration of Berlin and it developed into the Soviet efforts to abrogate the status of the city. The USSR's attempts to gain control of West Berlin ignore the right of the Western powers to be there, a right derived from the wartime conquest and subsequent occupation of Germany. The arrangements made between the Allied powers after Germany's defeat merely established an administration on the basis of the original right deriving from conquest. An interpretative negotiation or renegotiation of such right cannot alter the basis of this title.

As was pointed out earlier, the status of both Germany and Berlin was defined by the European Advisory Commission in a document signed in London on September 12, 1944 (Appendix I). It projected Greater Berlin as an area to be occupied and administered jointly by all three powers, independent of the Zones of Occupation which were to be established in Germany proper at the same time. Therefore, any communist claim that Berlin is part of the territory of the Soviet-occupied zone is patently invalid. This situation was not fundamentally changed when France was admitted on July 26, 1945, to partnership in the occupation arrangements for Germany and Berlin. A French Zone in Germany and a French Sector in Berlin were authorized with Soviet agreement on condition that the French territories would be carved out of the areas assigned to Great Britain and the United States. The document defining the occupation zones in Germany and Berlin was supplemented at the Potsdam Conference.

The Potsdam Agreement (Appendix IV) stipulated that local government was to be developed immediately in Germany in accordance with democratic principles. Elections were to be held as soon as possible for regional, provincial and state governments. The occupation authorities granted the democratic rights of assembly and public discussion as prerequisites for the establishment of the democratic political parties they had pledged themselves to encourage.

Although a central goverment was not established at the time of the

Potsdam Agreement, all of Germany was to be treated as one economic unit by the occupying powers. The Allied Control Council for Germany was established on November 14, 1944, as the supreme authority for Germany by the European Advisory Commission and was to be responsible for supervising all essential German administrative departments which were to centralize the control of finance, transportation, communication, foreign trade, and industry.

The Potsdam Agreement also indicated that Germany was ultimately to be restored as a single nation. In fact, the Agreement envisages a united Germany when it speaks of a "peace settlement for Germany to be accepted by the Government of Germany." At the end of the war, the Soviet government favored a single Germany. This was expressed by Premier Stalin, Soviet chief of state, in his Proclamation to the People on May 8, 1945, in which he assured the world that the Soviet Union did "not intend to dismember or destroy Germany."

Thus, the military allies, Great Britain, France, the United States and the USSR became the trustees for a new postwar Germany that was to be domocratically self-governed and ultimately reunited. The trusteeship was located in the traditional national capital, Berlin, more than 100 miles inside the Soviet Zone, and much nearer the Oder-Neisse line provisionally marking the administrative eastern border of the Soviet Zone than it was to its western boundary. Premier Stalin had expressly approved the basic agreement between the four powers that Berlin was to be a joint responsibility and, furthermore, was to be administered as a unit. No Soviet voice was heard at that time suggesting that Berlin should be under the sole control of the USSR.

To occupy Berlin as agreed, however, the Western powers had to possess all the rights inherent in their authority to transport troops and supplies to their respective sectors. Premier Stalin confirmed this right on June 18, 1945, when he acceded to a cable of June 14th from United States President Truman stipulating, among other things, the "free access by air, road and rail from Frankfurt and Bremen to Berlin for United States forces."

The Soviet premier, by promising to take all necessary measures to implement President Truman's express injunction, laid the foundation for the agreement made ten days later between Great Britain, the United States and the Soviet Union concerning the allocation of specific roads, rail lines and air lanes to be used by the Western powers between the Western Zones of Occupation and Berlin. These arrangements were made even more precise by the specific actions of the Allied Control Council in Berlin. In fact, it was these guarantees that covered the entry of United States troops into Berlin on July 1, 1945. Since then, the right of free access has been confirmed by constant usage. It was again recognized by the Soviets in the Jessup-Malik agreement of May 4, 1949, which ended the Berlin blockade. The Berlin airlift, which so successfully circumvented the blockade, is described in Chapter V.

The rights of access and supply of the Western powers in Berlin also covered the rights of the civilian populations in their sectors. It is the responsibility of the occupying power under internation law to guarantee the existence of the peoples in its charge. The special political status accorded Berlin and the general Potsdam principle to treat Germany as an economic unit confirmed the right of the people of Berlin to import goods from and export them to the Western Zones and beyond. Nevertheless, the Soviet government made Berlin more dependent on shipments from the West than would otherwise have been the case due to Marshal Zhukov's refusal (September, 1945) to supply the food that had previously been sent into Berlin as a routine matter. At any rate, the Western powers, with the tacit and perhaps involuntary encouragement of the Soviet government, assumed the responsibility for feeding the inhabitants of Western Berlin.

In light of events in subsequent years, it is apparent that Soviet actions respecting Berlin were not because Berlin is a vital material prize, but instead are due to a variety of considerations. Russian communist leaders likely believe that the existence of a free Berlin makes it impossible to consolidate their empire of Eastern European nations since a free Berlin holds out the hope for eventual freedom to these satellite countries. Free Berlin also makes it virtually impossible for the Soviets to solidify their regime in the Eastern Zone. The Soviets must keep a firm grip on East Berlin and the Soviet Zone in order to maintain their domination over their eastern European satellites.

It is conceivable that the Soviet Union believes its industrial power and military might are capable of being used as instruments of imperialistic policy against the Western democracies, as evidenced by its attempts to force the Western powers out of the city. Berlin is viewed as a weapon of political blackmail by the Russians as a means of disrupting the Western alliance with the Federal Republic of Germany.

Through the smoke screen of the crises over the Berlin problem, the Federal Republic is subjected to an impressive combination of military menace and political intimidation. The point to which this pressure is applied is the status of the Allied powers in West Berlin. Any change in Berlin's status as a result of Soviet pressure would be interpreted as a major victory for the Soviet Union in the world-wide struggle between the Communist bloc nations and the Free World. Such a change would not only mean a loss of prestige to be observed by all the world but could very well result in a decisive change in the balance of world power. Failure on the part of the Western Allies to honor their guarantees in Berlin would undoubtedly have serious repercussions around the globe.

Because of the complex historical, material and psychological factors which have made Berlin a symbol of Western resistance to Communism, the problem of Berlin as attested by the Infamous Wall has become, inevitably, a problem of the world.

Chapter IV

The Allied Kommandatura

The "Allied Kommandatura Berlin," a designation adopted at the fourth meeting of the Allied Commandants on August 1, 1945, was the principal Allied agency for the administration of Berlin. It consisted of the four Allied Commandants and their staffs. Based on specific terms contained in earlier arrangements, it was created separately by a formal agreement which defined its nature and functions in detail. It was signed by the commanding generals in Berlin on July 7, 1945.

Paragraph 7 of the Quadripartite Statement on Control Machinery—one of the earlier agreements—provides: "The administration of the 'Greater Berlin' area will be directed by an Inter-Allied Governing Authority, which will operate under the general direction of the Control Council, and will consist of four Commandants, each of whom will serve in rotation as Chief Commandant. They will be assisted by a technical staff which will supervise and control the activities of the local German organs." Other excerpts from the Quadripartite Statement are contained in Appendix V.

The Allied Agreement on Quadripartite Administration of Berlin which was signed on July 7 is contained in Appendix VI. Four days after the signing, the Commandants held their first quadripartite meeting and on July 25, 1945, the Allied Kommandatura was formally established in its permanent headquarters building in the United States Sector. In front of the building four poles flew the American, British, French, and Russian flags. The flag on the right pole rotated monthly, flying the flag of the country whose commandant was the Chief Commandant for that month.

Inside the Kommandatura building the four commandants sat at a rectangular table with the chairman at the head. If there was a British chairman, then a French representative would be on his right, across the table would be the Russian, and next to him the American. Beside each commandant sat his Deputy and his political adviser. Groups of experts were assembled around the room who wrote and passed notes to their chiefs or whispered suggestions.

The building also contained a number of smaller conference rooms. Here the committees convened to deal with routine work, issued agreed orders to the Berlin government, and worked on details of disagreed orders, instructions, and communications of great importance. These were then given to the deputies, who met twice a month in the main conference room, who screened them for presentation at the commandants' conference. In this plainly furnished room more international conferences have likely been held than in any other single room in the world today.

In the beginning, the Allied Kommandatura consisted of three levels of deliberative elements and a secretariat. The highest level was composed of the four Allied Commandants of Berlin. They were assisted by the Deputy Commandants, who relieved them of considerable work and who ordinarily met twice between conferences of the Commandants. The routine deliberative functions of the Kommandatura were the responsibility of a number of committees and sub-committees which were composed of experts on various phases of city administration. At first there were more than twenty committees, covering almost every aspect of life in a metropolis. In general, they were organized to correspond to the departments of the Berlin city government, each committee being responsible for supervising the activities of the corresponding government department. The administrative and clerical work was performed by the four Chiefs of Staff of the Allied Kommandatura and their secretaries.

To conduct the mass of business, the commandants were forced to reduce everything to bare essentials to prevent being overwhelmed by bitter international wrangling. Translation was unavoidable and time-consuming. Interpreters who were selected by the Kommandatura Chiefs of Staff to translate different parts of a discussion stood immediately behind their Commandants. However, when an American spoke, his statements were translated into French by the interpreter behind the French Commandant and into Russian from French by the interpreter behind the Russian Commandant. The Russian interpreter spoke excellent French and Russian but understood no English. To facilitate translation, each individual spoke in short sentences. The characteristic American "O.K." for approval or agreement was accepted and used by all the powers. On those rare occasions when the Russian representative agreed, he would assent by calling out "hokay." Usually, however, his decisions were "nyet."

The Kommandatura meetings were held at the highest level in the beginning but, because of the staggering volume of business to be transacted, the Deputy meetings were organized. At those meetings, the Deputies expressed the views and decisions of their commanders, made decisions and passed on to the Commandants those questions on which agreement could not be reached.

One of the first problems to be decided was when the meetings would be held. The Americans wanted to meet at nine o'clock in the morning. The British preferred eleven and the Russians suggested noon-time. American habits in Berlin were the same as in the United States. They were up early, had lunch at noon, dinner about six and worked at night only when absolutely required. The Russians rarely got to their offices before noon, ate lunch late in the afternoon, had dinner at ten, and worked in their offices till late at night. The British were in-between. They came to their offices in mid-morning, ate lunch at "oneish," had tea at four, and dinner at eight.

In actual practice, the Soviet delegation not only tried to starve Berlin, they, in fact, starved the Western Kommandatura conferees on several occasions. They started lengthy meetings shortly before noon—after they had had a late breakfast. The Western delegates, having breakfasted much earlier, were usually so famished by four or five o'clock after the long hours of often dull and meaningless argument that they would agree to almost anything, just to get a little time out to eat.

The first Kommandatura meetings were held on an informal basis. Rules of procedure evolved as time went on. Initially, the French had no vote but participated as observers. After the chairmanship had completed one rotation of Soviet, American and British officers, however, the French assumed their rightful place in all deliberations. The Russian representative was an expert on conference technique and used it effectively to his advantage. The French Commandant was a veteran soldier and a keen logician. The American and British Commandants were also career army officers and were expert on military tactics but not too familiar with ecomomics and politics. An amazing thing about the early Kommandatura meetings was that on one policy the free world and communist representatives were in complete agreement: they all wanted to give the Germans self-government—but for different reasons. There was little doubt that the British distrusted the Soviets; the French attitude toward the Russians was motivated by their sense of national honor; the Americans were eager to return home, and the Soviets hoped to incorporate Berlin and East Germany into the Soviet bloc through the German Communist Party more easily if the Westerners moved out.

National traits of character and psychology were likewise prevalent during the debates and discussions on the problems to be resolved. The American attitude was typically practical—"let's quit talking about it and do something about it." The French were quite impersonal and tended to apply logical considerations to the matters under discussion. The British leaned over backward to ensure fair play and absolute honesty. The Soviets spoke on for hours, hoping to crush all opposition by the sheer weight of words, and then they would endeavor to insert a different proposal. (This modus operandi is not unknown in American domestic politics.) The Russians did not demur from perverting the facts, figures, and words of other delegates if it suited their purpose.

The largest and one of the first problems of the Kommandatura was to prevent over three million Berliners from starving to death. Many sessions were concerned solely with formulating plans to feed the city. The Allies were fully convinced that since Russia had control of the agricultural area of Germany, it was her responsibility to provide the food. The Soviets, however, did not agree. They were antagonistic and aggressive as usual and produced figures to back up their statements which the Allies were unable to refute because they did not have the necessary data. The agreement, as finally worked out, provided that the Americans would furnish the food and the British the coal. Since the Western Allies had no stocks on hand, it was obviously the Russians' responsibility to continue feeding the inhabitants of Berlin until the Allied supplies arrived. The Americans proposed to turn over to the Russians the equivalent amount of food which had been supplied to the Western Sectors as soon as the Western stocks became available. The Soviets were not enthusiastic about this plan, professing to believe that the Americans would not keep their agreement and would eventually refuse to replace the food.

Needless to say, many difficult problems of supply, exchange and transportation had to be ironed out. For example—what kinds of food and what quantities did the Berliners need? What would be the equivalent of exchange in terms of different commodities? Would the Russians insist on replacing flour with flour and potatoes with potatoes? If not, what was the equivalent of flour in terms of milk, fresh vegetables, or meat?

When Berlin was captured, the Red Army had moved all herds of cattle to the eastern part of their Zone. It also imposed a levy on German farmers for potatoes and vegetables. The Red Army itself was well supplied and it was from those stocks that food was drawn to feed the Western Sectors. It was later replaced from American supply stocks.

Actually, the transporting of food into Berlin was one of the big problems. In return for live cattle delivered to them at the Bavarian border, the Russians would deliver meat in Berlin in the ratio of two pounds on the hoof to one pound of dressed meat. The Russians also had their way on the fish and meat ratio which was set at about two pounds to one in accordance with the book of regulations of the Red Army.

The British had heated arguments with the Russians in the Kommandatura meetings over the coal question. The Russians claimed that 7,200 tons of coal were required daily to provide the electric power for operating the subways and sewage systems, for electric lighting, and for commercial purposes. This figure included the American pro rata share since the Americans had no coal resources. The British protested, claiming that the gross amount was excessive, and stated they were having transportation difficulties and were heavily involved in other commitments in Germany. The Soviets were forceful in their demands and the British reluctantly agreed to make full deliveries.

They were not happy, moreover, about running their trains into the East Zone because of the Soviet confiscation policy. From the time they moved in, the Russians tore up railroad tracks and removed rolling stock, engines and railway equipment—all of which was shipped to Russia. Had they continued, the central German rail transport system would have been completely destroyed.

Some time later the British fell some 60,000 tons behind in their coal deliveries. They stated the delay was caused by labor problems in the Ruhr. The Soviet Commander suggested that some of the Berliners be put to work in the mines. But he did not explain why the Russians were 30,000 tons short in furnishing Berlin with the brown-coal briquettes which came from Chernowitz—in the region originally captured by U.S. troops and then handed over to the Russians.

Another difficulty confronting the Kommandatura delegates was the civilian ration allowance. Here the American and Russian ideas clashed sharply. The Russians claimed that the rationing system which they put into effect after entering Berlin was the same as in Moscow. It had five categories ranging from 1248 to 2485 calories per day per person. The Russian philosophy was to reward the productive worker, the political leader, and the government official. It was in strong contrast with the humanitarian approach of the Americans which was to meet the individual's physical needs. The Americans naturally protested the scanty allowance in the lower categories. When the Russians replied that the Berlin ration was the same as in Moscow, the Allies quickly demonstrated that this was not a valid argument. While the ration might have been the same, unrationed food could be purchased at free markets in Moscow in addition to the basic allowance. Berliners, civilians and city officials alike, were not permitted to obtain fruits, vegetables, or any other food from the countryside around the city because it would interfere with the purchasing or requisitioning of food supplies for the Red Army. Finally, after many arguments, the Soviets agreed to lift the restriction and permit the people to leave the city to get what food they could. The agreement never became an official document but Berliners took the train or walked out into the country and returned with sacks and shopping bags to the extent of about one hundred tons of fresh vegetables daily. Eventually, the Allied Control Authority raised the lowest category from 1248 to 1500 calories.

Food, fuel, and health problems were further complicated by the arrival of refugees from Russia, Poland and Czechoslovakia—deported Germans returning to their Fatherland—many of whom claimed to be Berliners although they could not prove it. With all roads and railroads leading into Berlin, the refugees flocked in by the thousands, reportedly bringing in about 25 per cent of the city's diseases, including typhus. The Soviets tried to re-route the trains around Berlin but, since it was the center of the rail system, it was not possible.

For once the Kommandatura was in full accord. They joined in press and radio announcements urging refugees to stay away because of disease and lack of food. Permits were no longer issued to enter the city, but efforts to restrict the flow were only partially successful. All that could be accomplished was to control the people on arrival, feed them one meal at night, and ship them out the following day. Some 300,000 persons are reported to have passed through Berlin in that manner between August and December, 1945.

The black market presented another thorny matter for the Kommandatura to resolve. In West Germany the medium was cigarettes, in Paris—gasoline, in Rome—food. But in Berlin, it was the barter market wherein a number of barter points was used for the sale or exchange of clothing, jewelry, and personal items. Barter was intended only for civilians who would swap luxury goods for food, if available, or clothing, ski equipment or furniture for overcoats, suits, shoes, etc. In order to exercise some degree of city control, each of the Sectors was authorized to establish at least one barter market with an official appraiser. Initially, currency was permitted to be used in a transaction only in an emergency. In the Tiergarten, in the British Sector, the Germans disposed of everything imaginable, from silver candelabra and valuable paintings to kitchen utensils and bicycles.

Surprisingly, the Soviets approved of the barter markets and apparently favored free trade despite its inconsistency with the communist economic system. Although Allied soldiers were supposed to keep out of the barter markets, the Russians let their troops in—but not to sell, only to buy. By then it had been agreed barter items could be purchased with currency. The secret of the sudden wealth of the Soviet troops was soon discovered. Plates for printing invasion money had been brought to Berlin by the Western Allies but, since there was enough money in circulation, they were not used. The Russians, who had duplicate plates, began printing notes at a rapid rate. Since this money could not be sent back to Russia, it was used by their troops who were encouraged to buy commodities and send them back to Russia. As wartime shortages gradually disappeared and barter items became fewer, the barter markets faded out of existence.

Variety was the norm at the Kommandatura conferences. With

thousands of details to consider in the administration of Berlin and with the Russians always questioning the proposals of the West, there was never a static moment.

Soon after the Soviets withdrew from the Allied Control Authority for Germany in March, 1948, they initiated a campaign of harrassment at all levels of the Kommandatura, from the Commandants' conferences to the sub-committee meetings. In April, the Soviet delegation began a series of tirades accusing the Western Allies of preventing the operation of the Kommandatura and attempting to dissolve the quadripartite government of Berlin.

That same month the Soviets started their campaign to break down rail and road communications with Western Germany. Under the guise of technical difficulties, the Russians exerted more and more control over the operation of the railroad. Checkpoint procedures were made more complicated and time-consuming. Passes were not honored, and soon Russian guards were tramping through passenger trains checking all passengers and inspecting all luggage—and always at night. When orders were issued that Soviet guards would not be permitted on passenger trains, the Russians refused to let the trains move. This same inspection procedure was applied to freight trains and, like passenger trains, they soon ceased to run. Military rail traffic between Western Germany and Berlin thus came to an end.

Similar obstructionist tactics were applied to road traffic. Traffic on the main highway between Berlin and the West, the Autobahn, was frequently "blocked for repairs" and traffic stopped. It would be reopened later only to find a bridge needed repairs so traffic would have to make a long detour over a second class road. The Autobahn was finally closed to all Western traffic. The Soviets' excuse for their actions was that they were looking for forbidden merchandise and cargo, black market operators and unauthorized travellers. With rail facilities stopped and road traffic unreliable, the Western Allies had already begun to use aircraft to carry passengers and freight in and out of the city. The coming airlift had already cast its shadow over Berlin.

Finally, on June 16, 1948, after more than thirteen hours of continuous but useless debate, the Soviet representatives walked out of the Kommandatura.

During the next several months, the Western Commandants and their staffs met unofficially at one of the three unilateral headquarters and continued to perform the essential functions of the Allied administration. However, on December 21, 1948, the three Western Commandants officially proclaimed the Kommandatura to be operative but left the door open for Russian participation (see Appendix VII). Except for reducing the number of committees and agencies, the general structure of the Kommandatura remained unchanged. Business and decision making followed the earlier procedures. Actions initiated at the sub-committee or committee level were passed up to the Deputy Commandants who were authorized to make decisions in many areas. Where there was disagreement among the Deputies and on certain important matters of policy on which only the Commandants could act, the issues were passed up to those officers.

The creation of the West German government in 1948 and 1949 necessitated the preparation of certain West German and Allied agreements. The Basic Law was designed as the provisional constitution of the West German Federal Republic. The Western Allies negotiated three documents:

> The Occupation Statute for Germany, which defined the occupational powers under the then new Allied-West German arrangement.
>
> The Trizonal Fusion Agreement, which effected complete amalgamation of the three Western Zones of Occupation and provided for the creation of the Allied High Commission for Germany as the Allied governing authority to exercise occupation functions.
>
> And, the Charter of the Commission, which defined its organization and function.

From these documents it was obvious that the Western Allies were unwilling to include Berlin in the Federal Republic of Germany as a separate constituent state. Hence, Berlin was treated independently. On May 14, 1949, two days after the lifting of the Berlin blockade, the three Western Commandants signed and issued the "Statement of Principles Governing the Relationship Between the Allied Kommandatura and Greater Berlin," which defined the authority and functions of the Western Allies in the city. (See Appendix VIII.)

The "Statement" specified that, subject only to specific limitations, Berlin was to have full legislative, executive and judicial powers in accordance with the Temporary Constitution of 1946 or any subsequent constitutive act adopted by the city government and approved by the Allied Kommandatura. The Western Allies reserved the rights of maintaining relations with foreign countries, protecting, and preserving the prestige of the Allied forces, preserving respect for the constitutional system of the city, and averting restrictions on the freedom of speech, press, assembly, and association until these rights would be guaranteed by the Berlin constitution.

Under the "Statement," the city government was empowered, after notifying the Kommandatura, to legislate and act in those fields reserved to the Western Allies, such action being permitted if it would not be contrary to decisions taken by the occupation authorities themselves or was not inconsistent with Kommandatura decisions. In actual practice, the city government was permitted to function in those areas reserved to the Allies with the approval of the Allied Kommandatura. In March, 1951, an "Instrument of Revision of Statement of Principles, 1951" was issued which modified the 1949 Statement and gave additional responsibility to the Berlin city government. (See Appendix IX.)

As the Berlin government grew in strength and stability, the Allied Kommandatura diminished its active participation in the administration of the city. The Kommandatura tailored its staff to its new role, eliminated committees and reduced its legislative review activities. It continues to represent Allied authority respecting the city of Berlin. While the formal governing action of the Western powers has greatly declined and practically all public administration in West Berlin is conducted by German officials, the Allied Kommandatura is still the repository of Allied responsibility until the Berlin problem is resolved.

It is interesting to note that the oldest World War II Allied occupation agency which is still in existence is the Kommandatura. All the others, including the Allied Control Commissions in various Axis European nations, the Allied Control Council and the Allied High Commission for Germany, and the Far Eastern Commission and the Allied Council for Japan, have been disbanded. None of the others operated as a quadripartite agency and later as a tripartite agency. Further, the Allied Kommandatura has dealt with an administration having theoretical jurisdiction over the entire city of Berlin, but yet was able to carry out its responsibilities only in the Western Sectors. Directives and regulations which pertained to all Sectors were issued by the Kommandatura, but where they applied only in the Western Sectors, they were co-ordinated and issued unilaterally in each Sector.

Currently, the Allied Kommandatura consists of the Commandants, their Deputies, the secretariat and a number of committees. Since the withdrawal of the Soviet members, the meetings have been conducted in a businesslike manner. No longer do the conferees have to contend with lengthy Communist political orations, parliamentary abuse and badgering tactics. The discussions are held with the object of resolving the issues as expeditiously and correctly as possible. More informal meetings are taking place than formerly. Finally, many Allied-German sessions are now being convened, which has resulted in establishing closer relations between the Kommandatura and various elements of the Western Allies with the German officials of the Berlin city government.

The withdrawal of the Soviet delegation in 1948 and the proclamation of the Tripartite Statement of Principles in 1949 and 1951 have raised a number of issues concerning the legal status of the present Kommandatura. There is no question of the legal right of the Western Allies to remain in Berlin since it is founded on the definite agreements made during 1944 and 1945 by the quadripartite Allied powers relating to the occupation of Germany and the control machinery for Berlin and Germany. The absolute right of the Western Allies was not based on the continued operation of either the Allied Kommandatura or the Allied Control Council.

It has therefore been maintained that none of the four powers could legally evict any of the others from Berlin. Further, no occupation power has the authority unilaterally to change the existing basic agreements which affect the other powers. The withdrawal of any of the powers could only be accomplished by new agreements entered into at the governmental level which would modify or rescind existing agreements.

As a result, the continued legal existence of the Allied Kommandatura was not changed by the Soviet walk-out. Moreover, such disassociation has not endangered the rights of the Western Allies to remain and discharge their responsibilities in West Berlin on a tripartite basis and on a Sector basis as well. The voluntary absence of the Soviet representative of the Kommandatura does not nullify the obligations of the other members to continue the operation of the Kommandatura.

It should be noted that the right of a Sector Commandant to exercise occupational authority in his Sector must be differentiated from his right as a member of the Kommandatura to participate in the control of all Berlin. The suspension of four-power operation of the Kommandatura in no way affects his right to remain in Berlin and to control his Sector.

From a legal viewpoint the Allied Kommandatura must remain in being as long as it exercises control over the Berlin city government. But under present conditions, it is not possible for one Commandant (Soviet) or three Commandants (Western Allies) acting together to administer the entire city.

If the Kommandatura were abolished, the 1950 Berlin city government would be forced to restrict its activities to the Western Sectors of the city as at present, even though it legally has the right to control the entire city. A new agency composed of representatives of the Western powers would have to be created which would be limited in authority to the Western Sectors. This would present no great legal problem provided the city government and the Western Sectors were one and the same area.

The situation where the Soviet delegation voluntarily absented itself from a legally constituted quadripartite agency, the Allied Kommandatura, in 1948 is similar to that which existed when the Soviet member voluntarily absented himself from the United Nations Security Council in June, 1950. Despite the fact that the Soviet delegate was not present, the Security Council continued to function. The Soviets questioned the legality of the actions taken by the Security Council without their concurrence, based upon the requirement for unanimity of the permanent Council members. The Council held that the voluntary absence of one of its members did not constitute a veto but was regarded as an abstention. The actions taken by the Security Council have been considered legally correct.

The Security Council situation might be regarded as establishing a precedent for the Berlin Kommandatura problem; in which case, the absence of the Soviet member could have no effect on Kommandatura actions subsequent to his walk-out. Actually, he is free to return at any time, but the terms and conditions under which he might return would most likely be determined by political considerations favorable to the USSR. Among these would be a return to the rule of unanimity. The Western Allies made a number of changes in the Kommandatura and adopted new procedures after the Soviet walk-out. These included the Statement of Principles for Berlin, 1949, and its 1951 revision, and an Agreement on a Revised Internal Procedure for the Allied Kommandatura. This latter document changed the voting procedure from the rule of unanimity to one of majority rule. Just as the use of the unilateral veto by the Soviet member of the United Nations Security Council has been so important to the Russians, so will it likely be as important to them to reinstate the unanimity rule as one of their conditions to return to the Kommandatura.

At the present time, the Western Allies are faced with a number of extremely weighty questions concerning the future status of the Allied Kommandatura. Would it be desirable to place the Kommandatura on an inactive status subject to reactivation to continue the quadripartite relationship, but, in the meantime, to replace it with a tripartite agency or a council of Western diplomatic representatives? What would be the resultant effect on East-West relations if the West took such action? What would happen if France should withdraw her troops from Germany and West Berlin and enter into a bilateral agreement with Germany? These and many more questions of similar nature must be answered by the four powers and West and East Germany in relation to their national policies before the Berlin question can be resolved.

Chapter V

The First Berlin Crisis

Prelude to the Berlin Blockade

A year after the surrender of the Nazi forces the German economy still lay in semi-chaos. Not one of the Zones was self-supporting. The United States renewed its effort to implement the Potsdam Agreement that Germany was to be treated as an economic unit. It proposed prompt establishment of central German administrative agencies, free trade between Zones, and a balanced program of imports and exports. The British agreed immediately but the French insisted that the Saar be excluded. The Soviets, using the French condition as a pretext, rejected the entire proposal.

At a speech in Stuttgart on September 6, 1946, U.S. Secretary of State James F. Byrnes stated that the Allied Control Council was neither governing Germany nor allowing Germany to govern itself. He explained the impending economic merger of the British and American Zones and laid down a positive economic program for all Germany. This included drastic fiscal reform to prevent ruinous inflation, and the organization of transportation, communications and postal service throughout the country without regard to zonal barriers, and a central administrative department for agriculture to improve production and distribution of food. He further stressed the importance of permitting Germany to increase industrial production and organize the most effective use of her raw materials, granting that Germany had to share her coal and iron with the liberated countries of Europe.

In the fall of 1946, the British and American Zones were merged for economic purposes. Hoping that differences with the Soviets could be resolved, the French held back. The Soviets, however, remained adamant. At the fifth session of the Council of Foreign Ministers of the four occupation powers, held during November and December, 1947, the Western delegates concluded that agreement with the

Soviets could be reached "only under conditions which would not only enslave the German people but would seriously retard the recovery of all Europe."

Soviet imperialistic objectives in Europe had become increasingly apparent. The first was to firmly establish Communist regimes over all areas of eastern and central Europe which the Red armies had occupied during and at the end of the war. The second and larger aim was to extend Communist domination over western and southern Europe. The Soviets were actively supporting an aggression against Greece, euphemistically called a civil war. They were pressing Turkey for concessions which would jeopardize its independence and open the way for further Soviet expansion into the Mediterranean area and beyond. In western Europe, they were counting on economic stagnation and political paralysis to set the stage for Communist takeovers.

In March, 1947, the United States, in an effort to curb Soviet expansion, extended economic and military aid to Greece and Turkey and proclaimed a general policy of such aid to other nations resisting overt or covert aggression. This policy became known as the Truman Doctrine.

In a speech at Harvard College in June, 1947, U.S. Secretary of State George C. Marshall set in motion the great co-operative European recovery program. The central conflict of purpose between the East and the West was set forth in December 1947 in Secretary Marshall's Report to the Nation:

> The issue is really clear-cut, and I fear there can be no settlement until the coming months demonstrate whether or not the civilization of western Europe will prove vigorous enough to rise above the destructive effects of the war and restore a healthy society. Officials of the Soviet Union and leaders of the Communist Parties openly predict that this restoration will not take place. We on the other hand are confident in the rehabilitation of western European civilization with its freedoms.

The nations of western Europe responded to the Marshall Plan with vigor and enthusiasm. The next several years witnessed the economic recovery of Europe, including the Western Zones of Germany. During this period, West Germany began political reconstruction on a democratic basis. On March 6, 1948, with the concurrence of Belgium, the Netherlands and Luxembourg, the Western Allies agreed to combine their Zones economically and politically. They agreed also on a new Occupation Statute which, while reserving essential powers to the Allies, enabled West Germans to participate in the community of free peoples through a federal government of their own choosing.

Developments inside Berlin during the year 1947 dramatically recorded the deepening crisis in East-West relations. Efforts to conduct effective Four Power control over Germany had failed and the Western Allies had organized their Zones—independent of Russian approval or disapproval—into a viable unit which outlined the future West German Republic. The failure of Four Power control was demonstrated when the Soviet delegation walked out of the Allied Control Council on March 20, 1948. The Soviet Union's rejection of participation in the Marshall Plan and the Communist coup in February 1948 in Czechoslovakia had eliminated the remaining avenues of co-operation between the East and West.

For Berlin, the most pressing problem was the city's position in the new system of two rival currencies on German soil. Monetary experts of the Western Allies and Soviets had been engaged in protracted negotiations in an endeavor to achieve agreement on an urgently needed currency reform for all of Germany. When it was evident that no agreement could be reached, the Western Allies prepared a currency reform for their three Zones, electing to stabilize the area under their control even at the expense of further deepening the division of Germany. Originally, Berlin, much less its three Western Sectors, was not seriously considered in the West German currency reform area. However, inclusion of Berlin in the Soviet currency bloc would have been considered abandonment of the city by the Western Allies.

Confidence in the Reichsmark had fallen so low that it had almost ceased to be used as currency—even in the black market. Coffee, butter and cigarettes were the preferred medium of exchange at fantastic values which bore no relation to their legal price. A single American cigarette had the purchasing power of a day's pay for the average worker.

On June 18, 1948, the Western military governors announced a reform basic to West Germany's economic recovery: the substitution of a sound currency, the Deutschemark (or D-mark), for the inflated Reichsmark. Three days later the Soviets countered with a currency reform in the East Zone which they attempted to force on all four Sectors of Berlin. The Western Allies had not insisted on introducing new German currency into Berlin as long as they shared with the Soviet Union control of the amounts of old currency issued. As a result of the Soviet action the Western powers then extended their currency to the three Western Sectors of Berlin where East-marks and West-marks were declared valid on a one-to-one basis. The Soviets, however, ruled that only East-marks were valid in the East Sector. It was inevitable that the situation wherein two currencies in circulation in adjacent East and West Sectors, supposedly equal but actually of vastly different market value, could not survive. Subsequently, only the West-mark was generally accepted in the three Western Sectors—and another major step had been taken toward the establishment of West Berlin as a separate entity.

During early 1948, the Soviet Union began to test the will and readiness of the Western Allies to remain in Berlin by harassing Allied traffic to and from Berlin. Western rights rested on implicit assurances rather than formalized agreements, particularly respecting overland traffic and movement of supplies for the civilian population. Berlin's geographic location deep in the East Zone presented many opportunities for the Russians to delay and interrupt traffic. On April 1, 1948, they imposed restrictions on all Allied rail and road traffic to Berlin. These were of such nature as to require the Western powers to decide whether or not to use military force to get their trains and convoys into Berlin. Back of their decision not to use force lay the risk of another major war.

On June 16, 1948, Soviet representatives walked out of the Berlin Kommandatura. One week later, when the West German currency reform was extended to West Berlin, the Soviets attempted to force the Berlin Assembly (then located in East Berlin) to reject the reform by starting riots of German Communists at the city hall. When the democratic representatives refused to be intimidated, the Soviet Union, on June 24, severed all land and water routes between Berlin and the Western Zones of Germany. It was an undisguised attempt to force the Western Allies out of Berlin and to starve the inhabitants of the city into acquiescence to Communist policy. This created the first major postwar Berlin crisis.

In response to this bold aggression against their rights and the freedom of the people of Berlin, the Western Allies would have been fully justified in using force to whatever degree necessary to reopen and maintain surface routes to Berlin. Instead, they chose the dramatic concept of supplying Berlin by air.

The fact that one type of route into the besieged city was not closed—the three twenty-mile-wide air corridors—was due to Allied diplomatic foresight in 1945 when the Quadripartite Agreement was negotiated defining the corridors and granting their free use under established rules. This Agreement effected the necessary coordination of operations of the four nations' aircraft in Berlin by creating a four-power Air Safety Center where all flight notices were posted. In March, 1948, the Russians requested that the Agreement be modified on the basis that several alleged infringements of its provisions by U.S. aircraft had been observed. Had these modifications been agreed to by the Western powers, night flying and instrument flying would not have been permitted through the corridors in and out of Berlin and the Berlin airlift could not have existed. Fortunately the Russian proposals were flatly rejected.

The Berlin Airlift

The task of supplying the necessities of life to the Western military community and to more than 2,000,000 Germans was the most spectacular supply operation in the history of aviation. General Lucius D. Clay, the U.S. military governor, with his British and French associates, ordered a joint enterprise which was to become famous as the "Berlin Airlift."

The responsibility for organizing and operating the initial airlift was assigned to US Air Forces in Europe (USAFE) under command of General Curtis E. LeMay (later Chief of Staff of the US Air Force). By utilizing all available transport aircraft (C-47's) and qualified pilots, 80 tons of milk, flour and medicine were flown into Tempelhof Air Base in Berlin from Wiesbaden Air Base on June 26. That same day, General LeMay had requested additional transports and crews from US Air Force Headquarters in Washington. In a matter of hours, aircraft and crews were winging their way to West

Germany from bases in the United States, Hawaii and Alaska. By July 20, there were fifty-four C-54's and 105 C-47's in operation, with a maximum daily airlift of 1,500 tons. British Yorks and Dakotas provided an additional 750 tons, but the combined total was still inadequate to meet requirements.

The daily airlift to support the American and French Sectors was approximately 3,000 tons and for the British Sector, 1,500 tons. It was obvious that the scale of operations had to be substantially increased. On July 23, the US Military Air Transport Service was ordered to send eight squadrons of C-54's (72 aircraft including replacements) and sufficient personnel to establish a task force headquarters to direct the Berlin Airlift under the operational control of USAFE. This involved approximately 2,500 men (including the headquarters staff), three crews per plane, traffic supervisors, and maintenance crews. Eight days later the U.S. airlift exceeded the 2,000-ton figure. It was fortunate that reserve stocks of food and supplies had been maintained in West Berlin which could be drawn on until the airlift was fully operational. The food stocks on hand were sufficient to last for thirty-six days and the coal stocks for forty-five days.

The new Airlift Task Force (Provisional) was activated on July 29 with headquarters at Wiesbaden. Major General William H. Tunner, who took command of the new organization, was a veteran of the airlift over the "Hump" to China during World War II. He also commanded the Combined Airlift Task Force which was established in October to merge the American and British operations. On the American side, the Berlin Airlift was a combined operation with the British and the French, and also a joint operation which involved the U.S. Army, Navy and Air Force. The Army Transportation Corps moved cargo to and from the planes; the Engineer Corps built additional runways on existing fields and constructed an entirely new airfield. Navy tankers brought enormous quantities of aviation fuel to Bremerhaven for the airlift and Navy crews and planes also participated in the 24-hour supply operation. By November, 1948, there were two Navy squadrons equipped with twenty-four R5D's (C-54's), with flying crews and maintenance personnel, taking part in the airlift.

By the end of September, the C-47's had been replaced by C-54's which could carry about ten tons, three times as much as the C-47's.

Although C-54's had been designed to carry passengers instead of cargo, they were quickly modified and became the workhorses of the airlift run. Replacement engines for the C-54's were flown in by a large Air Force C-74 Globemaster in August. Thirty tons of heavy engineering equipment were also delivered to Berlin before the C-74 returned to the United States. Five C-82's joined the airlift fleet in September and were used primarily to transport vehicles.

Of the 400 C-54's in active military service, 319 were employed in the airlift. The air crew replacement training program in the United States took 19 C-54's and about 75 more were normally grounded for maintenance, leaving between 209 and 228 operational for the 24-hour airlift operation. The British employed about 140 military and civilian aircraft, many of which were smaller than the C-54.

The initial shortage of trained maintenance personnel was relieved by the employment of German nationals. Very few aircraft were grounded for lack of spare parts and supplies after the first large shipment was flown in from the United States. C-54 engines were, however, in short supply. Because of the nature of the cargo, the planes soon became filthy from coal dust and flour and required considerably more washing and cleaning than was normal. In the winter, brooms and isopropyl alcohol were used to combat the ice, snow, and frost which accumulated dangerously on the planes on the ground.

Ground crews as well as air crews put in long hours, got little sleep and worked in foul weather. However, the arrival of additional personnel in July brought greatly needed relief. Unexpected rain and fog frequently covered Germany during August and September. These adverse flying conditions were largely surmounted by detachments from the Military Air Transport Services and the Civil Aeronautics Administration who installed and operated the latest weather, communication, and traffic control equipment.

From the very start, air traffic control was a first priority requirement because of the limited air space, capacity of the terminal airfields, and the large number of aircraft involved. The flight operations of the airlift crews flying by day and night, in clear weather and foul, made heroes of the American and British airmen. All flights had to remain within the three twenty-mile-wide air corridors that now provided the only access to Berlin. Extending out from Berlin as the hub, the shorter northern and central corridors terminated in the British Zone, while the longer southern corridor ended in the U.S. Zone. The U.S. aircraft flew into Berlin from their large bases at Wiesbaden and Rhein-Main at Frankfort in the early stages. As ground and air traffic built up at these bases, U.S. transports began operating over the shorter routes from the British Zone, first from Fassburg and then from Celle in December, 1948. Operationally, all these bases were near the entrances to the corridors and near the supply points for the commodities to be transported.

Within their respective Berlin Sectors, the British used Gatow while the Americans used Tempelhof. Tempelhof was the most difficult of the key airfields. Although quite large by ordinary standards, it was almost completely encircled by tall apartment buildings. A system of high intensity approach lights had been installed in the early winter of 1946 which necessitated the moving of several graves in the cemetery at the end of the runway to position the lights. While the Germans co-operated willingly, the Soviet propaganda machine ground out charges that the Americans were desecrating the dead. With the coming of the Airlift traffic, however, Tempelhof soon became overcrowded, even though additional runways were installed —and a new airfield was constructed at Tegel in the French Sector. Built from the rubble of Berlin by German men and women, working day and night, the new airfield was opened officially on December 7, 1948. U.S. planes loaded at Rhein-Main, Wiesbaden, Fassburg and Celle and unloaded at Tempelhof, Gatow and Tegel. The maintenance of these fields which were subjected to the continuous pounding of heavily loaded aircraft presented a major problem.

Although winter weather hampered the airlift flights, it never closed them down completely. Regardless of the weather, planes had to be flown exactly as prescribed—otherwise there would undoubtedly have been numerous air collisions. The designated routes avoided air traffic from other bases and provided a six-mile final leg into Berlin. Radio ranges, visual-aural ranges, radio and radar beacons and radar surveillance were employed to assist the pilot to maintain his correct flight position. The installation and operation of the Ground Control Approach (GCA) system was one of the most important factors which contributed to the success of the airlift. Properly trained GCA operators landed aircraft at three-minute intervals. GCA was used in all landings during marginal and instrument flying weather. If a pilot under GCA missed his approach,

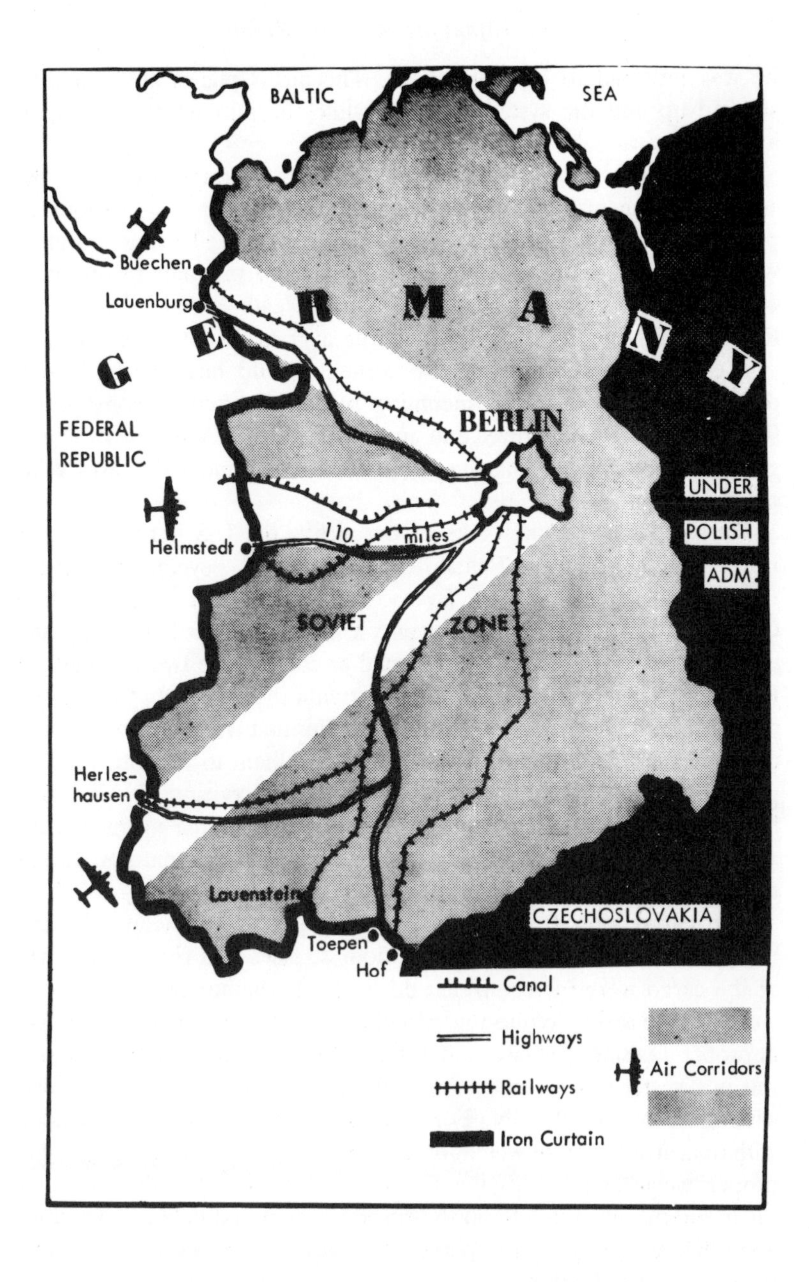
BALTIC
SEA
Buechen
Lauenburg
G E R M A N Y
FEDERAL
REPUBLIC
BERLIN
UNDER
POLISH
ADM.
110 miles
Helmstedt
SOVIET
ZONE
Herles-
hausen
Lauenstein
CZECHOSLOVAKIA
Toepen
Hof
Canal
Highways
Railways
Iron Curtain
Air Corridors

he was returned to his home base. The airlift planes could not be stacked up and the system delayed while the pilot went around for a second try.

During the winter, weather was the greatest single threat to the success of the airlift. Turbulence and icing were not as serious as predicted but fog proved to be a major hazard. During marginal weather—ceiling 200 to 400 feet and visibility one-half to one mile—it was impossible to accurately forecast weather changes for more than a half hour in advance. This was a great disadvantage since it was essential to know when an airfield would have to be closed down completely and the incoming planes diverted to some other field. Pilots, ground crews and maintenance men alike deserve the greatest credit for keeping the airlift functioning under the most difficult flying conditions.

During the first four weeks of the airlift, the U.S. Army and Air Force, together with the British Royal Air Force, developed an effective ground support system. By the end of July, the Transportation Corps was loading a block of seventy C-54's every six hours, day and night. Six truck-tractors were assigned to each of the two railheads at Rhein-Main and pulled a continuous stream of loaded ten-ton trailers to the airfield. The drivers returned the emptied trailers to the freight cars and picked up loaded trailers, bringing them to the airfield. The planes were loaded by Germans under the supervision of Air Force load-masters. The system became so efficient that the average turn-around time at the loading base was one hour and 25 minutes, and at the unloading base, 49 minutes.

The cargo aircraft were loaded in keeping with the weight and balance factors. Load distribution, floor stresses and proper tie-down of the cargo were factors which determined whether the aircraft was correctly balanced. While underloading might cause loss of tonnage, improper loading (which includes overloading) could very well result in disaster. As a result, commodities of high density were loaded with those of low density. For example, a C-54 completely loaded with macaroni would weigh only about 6,000 pounds. To get the proper weight and bulk, the C-54 would be loaded with sacks of sugar and macaroni to obtain the correct weight and balance. To eliminate delays in loading the planes, the cargo mixes were made when the trailers were loaded.

Every effort was made to increase the over-all payload. Equipment not essential to the operation of the C-54 was removed for a gain of about 2,500 pounds. Sacking cereals for air shipment was more economical than packaging. Dehydration reduced the daily requirement for potatoes from 900 to 180 tons.

On September 18, 1948, U.S. planes delivered a record 5,583 tons of coal to Berlin. The daily minimum airlift requirements, which were initially set at 4,500 tons, were increased to 5,620 tons on October 20. This increase resulted in an improved daily ration. This figure was broken down, in tons, as follows: food—1,435; coal—3,084; commercial and industrial items—255; newsprint—35; liquid fuel —16; medical supplies—2—for a total for the German population of 4,827 tons. For U.S., British and French military—763 tons; and for three C-54 daily passenger flights—30 tons.

Without coal Berlin could not have survived, and therefore it constituted two-thirds of all tonnage transported. Neatly sacked, it looked comparatively easy to handle but the abrasive dust soon permeated the interior of the fuselage, the wings and even the engine nacelles. Tarpaulins were laid on the floor of the fuselage and the sacks were lightly sprayed, but the coal dust still penetrated the aircraft structure. Finally, in February, the floors were sprayed by a sealing compound and the coal packed in multi-laminate paper sacks, and the dust problem was brought under control.

Food, the second largest item transported, included: flour, sacked grains, frozen meats, fish, potatoes, vegetables, cereals, sugar, fats, dairy products, coffee, cheese, yeast, and salt. The major food-handling problem was caused by the corrosive effect of the salt on aircraft control cables when it would seep through the plane floors. This was resolved by the use of British flying boats which had overhead cables treated against corrosion. Later, salt was transported in special cargo boxes in the bomb bay of converted RAF bombers and in outside containers attached to the fuselage of British Halton aircraft. Frozen foods and meats were moved so rapidly that very small spoilage loss was incurred. Pilferage, however, was a big problem because food was more valuable than money at that time.

Gasoline, oil, and lubricants were transported in fifty-five gallon metal drums in the beginning. This method was unsatisfactory because of the tonnage lost in the drums' weight, the necessity for steam cleaning the empty containers before re-use, and the time-consuming process of emptying the drums into permanent storage facilities. It was discontinued when a British fleet of chartered tankers took over the airlift of all liquid fuels. These tankers operated between the British bases and the Berlin airfields of Gatow and Tegel where underground storage facilities permitted discharging the cargo by gravity flow at a rate of 28.3 tons per hour. The daily delivery averaged about 550 tons.

Heavy equipment for airfield construction, medical supplies, rolls of newsprint, clothing, mail, parcel post, and raw materials to keep the city's industries alive were also airlifted into Berlin. Outbound cargo included machine tools and other manufactured items. Probably the most unusual supply drops during the airlift were started by Lieut. Gail S. Halvorsen, a MATS pilot, who dropped small parachutes of gum and candy to German children who waited near the end of the runway. This unofficial operation began in July and as time went on the crowds of children grew larger and larger. A logistics problem soon developed—finding enough handkerchiefs, old sheets, or articles of clothing from which to make the parachutes.

By January, 1949, the chief goal of the airlift had been accomplished—that of providing sufficient food for West Berlin. That month the food ration was increased from 1600 to 1880 calories a day per person. Meeting the coal requirements for the city was more difficult. Deliveries of coal during 1948 lagged except in September when the airlift concentrated on coal shipments. Nevertheless, enough coal was continuously brought in to provide the most essential services, although the rations of gas and electric power to the Germans had been severely curtailed. Monthly deliveries of coal climbed steadily during 1949 and reached a cumulative total on September 30 of 1,586,029 tons.

The operational efficiency of the airlift fleet steadily improved, peaking out in mid-April with the Easter achievement. On that day, 1,398 planes flew into Berlin carrying an all-time record of 12,904.9 tons. The Russians must have been impressed because less than a month later the Soviet authorities announced the end of the blockade of Berlin, effective 12 May 1949.

Thus, the eleven-month effort of the Soviets, supported by German communists, to force the people of Berlin into accepting communist rule and to absorb the city into the communist orbit through starvation, lack of fuel and unemployment failed—defeated by a technically complex and hazardous but none-the-less triumphant undertaking.

The airlift, however, continued to operate to build up reserve stocks until October 31, 1949. During the blockade period, American, British, and French air crews made 277,728 flights into Berlin, carrying 2,343,301 tons of food and supplies. At the peak of the airlift, planes were landing in West Berlin at the rate of one every forty-five seconds.

For the first few days after the blockade began, it was difficult for the Germans in the West Sectors to decide whether to throw in their lot with the Western Allies. Certainly there was no assurance that a prolonged effort to supply West Berlin by air was possible and, if the West abandoned Berlin, it would have been most unwise to have antagonized the communists. Even deciding to side with the West for a short period meant accepting certain obvious disadvantages and risks.

The Soviets tempted West Berliners by promising to provide them with all the necessities if they would register for rations in the East Sector. Under the leadership of the democratic politicians who were determined to rely completely on Western support—and by so doing bind the West more fully to its commitment—hesitant Germans of West Berlin soon gained a feeling of confidence and solidarity. Although they were preoccupied initially concerning the confused currency reform and later with the problems created by acute shortages of fuel, electricity, and food, they came to accept, and in a vague way to enjoy, their most unusual position as a beleaguered outpost of Western democracy. West Berliners became proud of their role as they identified themselves with the powerful Western forces whose airlift planes thundered overhead by day and by night. For the first time, they felt themselves accepted and appreciated as allies in the fight for a worthwhile cause.

Undoubtedly their rejection of Soviet communist totalitarianism was basic in their siding with the West. Probably not so much as an abstract theory but rather because they had experienced it and observed its operation intimately since the Red Army arrived in Berlin in 1945. In this frame of mind West Berliners learned to cope ingeniously with the myriad problems, inconveniences and hardships besetting them during the blockade, following the advice which they received from their own political leadership. In spite of the many problems involved, the vast majority of West Berliners refused to register for food rations in the East Sector. They refused to participate in communist-led demonstrations but they took part fully in mass-meetings called by Mayor Reuter to demonstrate and boost morale. They worked overtime when necessary and many walked long distances to work. With fuel scarce and electricity turned on only three hours out of twenty-four and at various times in the different sections of the Western Sectors, cooking and eating occurred at odd and unusual hours.

The experiences of the blockade forged a lasting bond of friendship among Berliners, Americans, and their Allies. Every noon the ringing of the Freedom Bell from the tower of the West Berlin city hall serves as a reminder to their common cause. This bell was a gift from millions of Americans including school children who voluntarily contributed to the fund to make and install it in the tower on October 24, 1950. It was inspired by the Liberty Bell in Independence Hall in Philadelphia which pealed the news of the American Declaration of Independence in 1776.

The question has been frequently asked: Why did not the Soviets try to stop the airlift? At first they probably believed it would not be possible to sustain West Berlin and the Allied forces in it by air alone. Later, they possibly thought that fog and hazardous winter weather would end the airlift. Perhaps the most influential factor was that they could not interfere with the airlift without shooting down Allied planes—an act of undisguised warfare which was too dangerous to risk.

The airlift did have its casualties, however. Seventy-two men, including thirty-one Americans, lost their lives in accidents. Their names are perpetuated on a soaring monument in front of Tempelhof Airport. A Berlin foundation, "Airlift Gratitude," provides scholarships for the children of these fallen airmen. If they wish, they may attend the Free University of Berlin as guests of the Free Berlin government. The university was born under the airlift when many teachers and students from the old University of Berlin situated in the Soviet Sector chose freedom in the Western Sectors. The new university held its first classes by candlelight in nine cold rooms in an old building during the airlift. Today the Free University of Berlin, with its more than 12,000 students, has become one of the world's great institutions of higher education.

While the spectacular operation of the airlift succeeded in defeating the Soviet object of forcing the entire city into the communist ranks, it did not prevent the perhaps permanent division of the city itself. The process of splitting the city which had been under way since the election of 1946 reached a climax. The functioning of the freely elected city officials was made impossible in the Soviet Sector. Riots were staged around the city hall; noncommunist city employees were dismissed in great numbers, and the activities of noncommunist parties and trade unions were severely restricted. In August and September, 1948, the communists prevented the City Assembly from holding its meetings by packing the hall with shouting demonstrators and creating riots in front of the building. The communist-controlled police of the East Sector made no attempt to preserve order.

On November 31, 1948, the communists called an extraordinary meeting of the City Assembly to which only the Socialist Unity Party (communist) and Communist-controlled masses and plant organizations sent delegates. This meeting voted the removal of the freely elected administrative board and appointed a new Communist board which was recognized two days later by the Soviet Commandant as the only legitimate city executive body. The regularly scheduled elections were held a few days later in the West Sectors —Soviet authorities prohibited them in the East Sector. The result of the free election was a clear endorsement of the men and parties pledged to resist Communist totalitarian threats. Ernst Reuter's Social Democrat Party received almost two-thirds of the votes cast. Barred from returning to the city hall in the Soviet Sector, the new parliament set up headquarters in West Berlin and elected Reuter as mayor. Legally, he was mayor of the entire city; actually, he could exercise authority only in its Western Sectors.

By the spring of 1949, it was evident that the airlift had defeated the Russian blockade. The Soviet Government, faced with the creation of the North Atlantic Treaty Organization and the failure of the Berlin blockade, signed a Four Power Agreement in New York on May 4, 1949, which provided in part:

> All the restrictions imposed since March 1, 1948, by the Government of the Union of Soviet Socialist Republics on communications, transportation, and trade between Berlin and the Western zones of Germany and between the Eastern and the Western zones will be removed on May 12, 1949. (See Appendix X.)

This article was implemented on May 9 by Order No. 56 of the Soviet Military Government and Commander-in-Chief of the Soviet occupation forces in Germany. It was reaffirmed, strengthened, and amplified the following month (June 20, 1949) by the Council of the Foreign Ministers of the Four Powers meeting in Paris.

Under the Paris agreement, the Soviet Union, together with the Western powers, undertook to ensure and facilitate free access to Berlin: "In order to improve . . . the movements of persons and goods and communications between the eastern zone and the western zones and between the zones and Berlin, and also in regard to transit. . . ." It was further stated, "the occupation authorities . . . will have an obligation to take the measures necessary to ensure the normal functioning and utilization of rail, water and road transport for such movement of persons and goods. . . ." (See Appendix XI.)

Chapter VI

The Second Berlin Crisis

Decade of Reconstruction and Bargaining

The termination of the blockade marked the end of the immediate Soviet effort to drive the Western Allies out of Berlin and to incorporate the city into the East Zone. The airlift victory was a serious setback to their offensive policy and did not change the fundamental dissatisfaction of the Russian regime with the presence of the Western powers in Berlin. While a decade of reconstruction and relative peace followed, the Russians began a new series of harassing actions in January, 1950. A "creeping blockade" designed to wreck, or at least hamper, the recovering economy of West Berlin was instituted. Persistent interference with the transportation and delivery of supplies, equipment and products from the West was combined with a violent propaganda campaign intended to intimidate the West Berliners.

Despite the harassment, the West Berliners proceeded energetically to rebuild their city and revive their industries. They cleared away war ruins and rubble and restored public parks and gardens. They re-equipped factories and power plants and built new ones. An immense new electric power plant, its enormous generators flown in part by part during the blockade, made West Berlin independent of communist-controlled sources of power.

Distance with its related handicaps made it difficult for industries in West Berlin to compete with those in West Germany and foreign countries. In 1955, the Soviets added to these problems by drastically increasing tolls on highway traffic between West Germany and Berlin. But through initiative, hard work and Marshall Plan aid (which now totals almost a billion dollars), West Berlin's industrial output grew rapidly. New office buildings, apartment houses and hotels sprang up. Stores and shops began to bulge with goods provided by the advanced technology and manufacturing techniques of the West. Free Berlin has again become Germany's greatest industrial city and the largest metropolis between Paris and Moscow.

The economic development of West Berlin following the end of the blockade has been little short of miraculous. In 1949, the city was in essentially the same state of ruin and devastation as when the fighting ended in 1945. During the blockade, unemployment in the Western Sectors was about 115,000 and the economy was at a low subsistence level. As a result of the currency reform, economic isolation and uncertainty about the future, the number had increased to around 300,000 in 1952. The following year, West Berlin was incorporated into the West German financial and economic system and unemployment declined rapidly. By 1959, it was down to around 40,000. Since 1961, it has been a problem to find enough manpower to fill West Berlin's needs.

At first the economic development of West Berlin trailed behind West Germany's by several years. Using a production scale of 100 for 1936, West Berlin's index for 1950 was 23 as compared with West Germany's 110. In 1955, West Berlin reached the 1936 index of 100 and was about 167 by 1961. During 1950-60, wholesale and retail trade doubled and tripled and exports increased about tenfold. During the blockade, as well as before and for a few years after, West Berlin economy depended almost entirely on American assistance. Beginning in late 1952, its increase was mainly due to the integration of West Berlin into the fast-growing West German economy and to a number of measures taken by the German Federal Republic to facilitate investments and expansion in Berlin. In addition, the government made unqualified contributions to a number of special projects which included extension of the subway, construction of an intracity autobahn, public housing and building programs.

Economic and financial ties between West Berlin and West Germany grew stronger despite the uncertain legal position of West Berlin in the German constitutional system. West Berlin was listed as one of the states in the federation in the Basic Law of 1949 which established the German Federal Republic; however, the Western Allies suspended this provision, stating that Berlin could not be governed by the German federal government. This was probably done to maintain their position that Berlin was not part of any of the four zones and therefore was not in the territory of the Soviet Zone and, further, that their own presence was not affected when the German Federal Republic was granted sovereignty.

Nevertheless, the Western Allies permitted a wide application of German federal law to West Berlin. The West Berlin constitution of 1950 provided that each federal law to be valid in Berlin had to be separately voted, if requested by the city parliament. This provision was later modified to permit the automatic reception of such laws by a comprehensive act. Except for such laws as those relating to the re-establishment of German armed forces, West Berlin has in fact been incorporated into the federation. There are some ambiguities, however. For example, federal ministries maintain branch offices in West Berlin to supervise the administration of federal laws; yet the decisions of the federal constitutional court are not applicable to West Berlin. West Berliners are not permitted to vote in elections for the German parliament but are permitted only to send an observer delegation selected by the West Berlin Assembly to Bonn. Yet, the federal lower house and many of its committees hold meetings in Berlin from time to time. The election of the German president in 1954 and 1959 also took place in West Berlin. Thus West Berlin, in spite of its geographical isolation, has become a de facto member of the German Federal Republic.

The political reconstruction of West Germany progressed rapidly even during the blockade. On September 1, 1948, the West German parliamentary Council convened in Bonn under the chairmanship of Dr. Konrad Adenauer, anti-Nazi former mayor of Cologne, to draft a provisional constitution (Basic Law). The Council completed its work in May 1949 and on August 14, 1949, the citizens of West Germany voted in the first free general election since 1932. On September 21, 1949, the Federal Republic of Germany came into existence with Dr. Adenauer, leader of the Christian Democratic Party, as its chancellor.

The formation of a freely elected, sovereign and internationally recognized German government in the former three Western Zones of Germany spurred the Soviet authorities to counter-action. On October 7, the Soviets set up their puppet regime in the Eastern Zone of Germany. With the support of the Soviet government and in further violation of the Four Power Agreements, the imposed East German regime proclaimed the Soviet Sector of Berlin to be its capital.

Early in 1950, the Soviet government began arming East German forces, at first under the guise of "People's Police" (VOPO'S). Protests of the Western Allies were rejected. By the end of 1953, East Germany, with only 17 million people, had 140,000 military personnel, including three mechanized divisions, an air force, and 10,000 armed police. This was in sharp contrast with the policy of the Federal Republic which, for a population three times that of the Soviet Zone, had only 150,000 regular state police, none of them under the jurisdiction of the federal government. Not until 1955 were there any armed forces under the Federal Republic.

In a series of actions in 1954 and '55, the Soviet authorities purported to grant full sovereignty to their East German puppet state. Among other moves, they transferred to it control of the borders between the Federal Republic and West Berlin and the Soviet Zone and East Berlin and over German traffic between the two areas. The Western powers emphatically reminded the Soviet Union that these arrangements did not alter its obligations under its prior and overriding agreements with them regarding Germany and Berlin.

In 1951, a special commission was set up by the United Nations to determine whether conditions were suitable for holding free elections throughout Germany. This U.N. commission was unable to complete its task because it was barred from the Soviet Zone of Germany and the Soviet Sector of Berlin. Thus, the Soviet Union, consistent with its behavior in all its satellites, once again refused to allow the test of public opinion to be applied in their area. This was but one more proof that the power of the regime in the Soviet Zone is maintained by the police apparatus of the Communist Party, backed by Soviet military forces. Since the East German regime was unlawfully created and does not rest on the consent of the governed but is kept in power backed by the military force of the Soviet Union, the Western nations have refused to recognize it—as have all other noncommunist countries.

The role of Soviet forces in maintaining communist power in East Germany became apparent in one of the most significant rebellions yet recorded against Russian tyranny and in which the great majority of East Germans and East Berliners participated. The long series of oppressive acts that kept the East Germans in a continuous state of agitation finally came to a climax in a violent explosion. The desperate shortages of food, housing and clothing, the payment of slave wages, the suppression of churches, the confiscation of farm lands, the failure to meet the quotas for labor output or farm crops were the underlying causes of the revolt. In addition, the Soviet regime had confiscated almost all private industrial and manufacturing enterprises and was about to curtail food rations and make a drastic cut in wages.

Of all the regime's actions, that which was most bitterly resented was the decree raising the Communist work "norms," the standards of productivity which workers were required to meet to earn their pay. Newspaper articles in the East German press which were designed to explain and justify the new work norms had the opposite effect and further inflamed the working population.

On June 16, 1953, some three hundred workers decided to demonstrate their protests against the increased work norms and pay cuts by marching to the Hall of Ministries. As the parade moved up Stalin Allee, its ranks were swelled spontaneously by other workers. Soon thousands of men and women left their jobs and joined the protest march. The demonstrators stormed the government ministry on the Leipzigerstrasse, calling for the Soviet puppet leader, Walter Ulbricht, to show himself. The strike quickly spread all over East Berlin.

The radio station in the American Sector was on the air and news of the rebellion spread throughout Germany. The East Berliners threatened to continue the strikes and demonstrations the next day unless their demands for free elections, reduced cost of living and working norms were met. Early on the morning of June 17, more than 100,000 East Berliners were milling around and chanting in the streets. The peaceful demonstrations for democratic liberties and reasonable working conditions became a full-scale revolt which swept into the East Zone.

Soviet authorities decreed a state of emergency. Pitched battles broke out in the streets with the East German police, who were soon joined by troops of the Red Army. Russian troops with their T-34 tanks charged into the crowds and the rebellion was crushed though the fighting continued for hours. In some cities of East Germany, Communist Party headquarters were burned to the ground, statues of Stalin overturned, political prisoners released from jail and Russian flags torn down and destroyed. Unarmed East Germans were no match for Russian tanks and machine guns, however, and many paid with their lives. The fact remains that it took Russian tanks and troops to quell the rebellion—just as they were required in Hungary three years later before that unco-ordinated but passionate uprising could be crushed.

One of the significant aspects of the June 17 revolt was that it was led and carried out by the industrial proletariat—construction workers, factory workers and other wage earners—the very people whom the Communists claimed particularly to represent. The revolt was in fact an uprising of the proletariat against the dictatorship of the proletariat.

West Berliners were prevented by Allied troops and West Berlin police from rushing into East Berlin to aid their countrymen in the fight. Although June 17, 1953, was established as a special day of commemoration, it was a bitter and lasting lesson to all Berliners that it was useless to rebel and try to take matters into their own hands unless the Western powers were willing to run the risks incident to changing the status quo division of the city. Thus, June 17 was a milestone in the postwar history of Berlin in its process of consolidating the city by dividing it. The Western Allies and leading political authorities such as Dr. Adenauer and Mayor Reuter concluded that successful reconstruction of a free Germany was possible only at the price of deepening the East-West split. How much longer the communist leaders of East Berlin would permit the bright light of progress of the West Sector to shine into the East Sector became a matter of considerable concern. The failure of the Communists to build and transform their area as the Western leaders had accomplished so successfully in their sections was all too obvious.

During the 1950's, the German Federal Republic took its place as a partner in the world of self-governing peoples. On May 26, 1952, the three Western powers signed contractual agreements ending the occupation of West Germany, to take effect when the Federal Republic was integrated into NATO, the Western European defense community. They reserved only the rights necessary to fulfill their obligations in regard to Berlin, the reunification of Germany, and a final peace settlement. They retained the right to station armed forces in Germany for defense of the Free World, of which the Federal Republic and Berlin formed a part. On May 27, 1952, they pledged themselves again to maintain armed forces in Berlin as long as needed and reaffirmed that they would treat any attack against Berlin as an attack upon themselves.

On the basis of the Protocol to the North Atlantic Treaty on the Accession of the Federal Republic of Germany, dated October 23, 1954, the Federal Republic assumed full partnership in the Atlantic defense community. After final ratification of the Protocol, the Federal Republic acceded to the treaty on May 5, 1955, when Germany was accepted into the Western European Union (Brussels Treaty) and the North Atlantic Treaty Organization. Germany agreed to limits on both armaments and independent military action. On its behalf, Chancellor Adenauer voluntarily undertook not to manufacture atomic, biological or chemical weapons. He also undertook not to produce long-range missiles, guided missiles, strategic bombers and large warships except with the approval of the Council of the Western European Union by a two-thirds vote. The Federal Republic placed all its military forces under NATO command; it is the only NATO member to have done so.

In the Joint Declaration by the Governments of the United States of America, the United Kingdom and France on the Three Power Guarantee for Berlin, dated October 3, 1954, it was stated:

> 5. The security and welfare of Berlin and the maintenance of the position of the Three Powers there are regarded by the Three Powers as essential elements of the peace of the free world in the present international situation. Accordingly they will maintain armed forces within the territory of Berlin as long as their responsibilities require it. They therefore reaffirm that they will treat any attack against Berlin from any quarter as an attack upon their forces and themselves. . . .

This collective reaffirmation of the unshakable Western determination to preserve the status of Berlin was an integral part of the Paris Treaties, which also provided for West Germany's membership in NATO. (See Appendix XII.) In these treaties, the Allies pledged to recognize only one German government and to support reunification. In return, the Federal Republic linked its most basic security requirements to the fifteen-country NATO alliance. No German general staff was established, and in NATO's complex network of international command and staff structure, inherently defensive in character, the United States plays the major role.

Further reflecting Germany's rejection of nationalism, the Federal Republic has become a strong supporter of the political and economic integration of Europe through the European Common Market, the European Atomic Energy Community and the European Steel and Coal Community. These Atlantic and European institutions leave no room for genuine fears of a new German supernationalism, particularly if Germany is permitted to reunite in peace and freedom.

After Premier Stalin's death and the Korean truce in 1953, the Western Allies resumed their efforts to obtain a peace settlement for Germany as a whole. Another fruitless meeting of the Foreign Ministers convened in Berlin on January 25, 1954, to consider the "Eden Plan," which sought to secure the reunification of Germany based on free general elections. The Soviets made plain their resolve to keep East Germany in captivity and to permit its unification with West Germany only under conditions which would favor the extension of Communist control over all Germany.

The Austrian peace treaty, formally designated as the "Austrian State Treaty," to which the Soviets finally acceded in May, 1955, generated new hopes. On July 23, 1955, at the Heads-of-Government Conference at Geneva, a directive of the Heads of Government of the Four Powers to the Foreign Ministers stated:

> The Heads of Government of France, the United Kingdom, the U.S.S.R. and the U.S.A. . . . instruct their Foreign Ministers to continue the consideration of the following questions . . . taking account of the close link between the reunification of Germany and the problems of European security . . .
>
> The Heads of Government, recognizing their common responsibility for the settlement of the German question and the reunification of Germany, have agreed that the settlement of the German question and the reunification of Germany by means of free elections shall be carried out in conformity with the national interests of the German people and the interests of European security.

At the subsequent Foreign Ministers Conference, convened in October, 1955, the Western powers submitted proposals in full harmony with that directive.

This action, which seemed to herald a possible rapprochement on the German problem, was frustrated once again when the Soviet authorities nullified the directive completely by insisting that the unification of Germany take place not on the basis of nation-wide free general elections but through "negotiations between two German states."

This was intended to enable the Soviets to retain a decisive voice in German affairs. Since central Germany is a puppet of the Soviet government, "negotiations" between the two parts of Germany simply meant that the Federal Republic would actually be bargaining with the agents of the Soviet government without the assistance of the three Western powers. This unproductive conference adjourned November 16, 1955

In 1956 and '57, President Eisenhower and other Western leaders sought further clarification of Soviet views. Responses from Moscow were rigidly negative. In 1957, Soviet Premier Bulganin made an attempt to entice the Federal Republic into negotiations with the Soviet Zone regime, at first on trade matters and then on the establishment of a loose confederation between the two parts of the country. This latter proposal had also been publicly advanced by the East German puppet president. Since no provision was made for central authority being established for the nation as a whole or for free elections, the Federal Republic rejected it. This decision was supported not only by the Christian Democratic Union, the party in power, but by the entire Social Democratic opposition.

A further attempt was made by the Western powers and the Federal Republic on July 1, 1957, to couple discussion of German reunification with security measures which would reassure the Soviet government. Again the Soviet authorities resisted any arrangements involving reunification on the basis of free elections. In December, 1957, the Soviet Union called for a new summit conference. After consultation with NATO members, President Eisenhower agreed to participate provided that the groundwork was laid through diplomatic channels and the Foreign Ministers. The exchanges which followed yielded no progress.

This, then, was the stalemate between the Four Powers in Germany until the end of 1958, when the Soviet government launched the second Berlin crisis.

The Second Berlin Crisis

In the winter of 1958, the period of reconstruction and relative calm came to an abrupt end and the Berlin problem suddenly erupted into an acute Berlin crisis. The time had arrived when Premier Khrushchev and his German "governor," Ulbricht, decided to force the issue and settle the problem which Khrushchev had earlier described as "a bone in our throat." The attack began with a speech on November 10 in which Khrushchev publicly denounced the Potsdam Agreements, especially those parts pertaining to the Four-Power status of Berlin. It was followed by another abusive and threatening speech on November 26 and a note to the Federal Republic of Germany and the Western powers on November 27.

In the note the Soviet Union stated that it considered null and void all its agreements with the Western Allies as to Berlin and demanded the withdrawal of all Western military forces from the city. It proposed to make Berlin a demilitarized "free city." Respecting reunification of Germany, the note proposed that the two "German States" enter into negotiation looking forward to a confederation —but without free elections in the East Zone. Excerpts from the note are contained in Appendix XIII. A deadline of six months was set, after which, if its demands had not been met by the Western powers, the Soviet government threatened to sign a peace treaty with the so-called German Democratic Republic (i.e., the Soviet Zone) and turn over to it physical control of Berlin, including all access routes to Berlin.

This note, like so many other documents emanating from Moscow, was replete with omissions and distortions. To begin with, the note ignored the fact that the presence of the Four Powers in Berlin is rooted not in negotiations between them but in original rights of the Western Allies as belligerent occupants of Germany. The Soviet Union cannot take away the rights and obligations of the Western Allies to remain in and protect Berlin since they were not conferred by the Soviet Union but are based upon the Nazi surrender. These rights include the right of access to Berlin. Moreover, the Soviet Union cannot unilaterally modify or annul its agreements with the

Western Allies as to Berlin, including its guarantees of access to Berlin since under international law, additional treaty rights based on occupation arrangements cannot be modified unilaterally—the consent of all powers concerned is required.

On December 14, 1958, the Foreign Ministers of France, Great Britain and the United States again pledged themselves to maintain all their rights in Berlin. (See Appendix XIV.) In its reply of December 31, the United States rejected the Soviet demands and stated that it could not embark on discussions with the Soviet Union "under menace of ultimatum." It nevertheless inquired if the Soviet Union were ready to enter into discussions among the Four Powers on the question of Berlin "in the wider framework of negotiations for a solution of the German problem as well as that of European security." Similar replies were sent by France and Britain.

The people of Berlin also rejected the Soviet notes. In December, 1958, elections to the city parliament were held in West Berlin. The vote of the SED (Socialist Unity Party of Germany), which campaigned for the Communist "free city" plan, amounted to less than 2 per cent. Participation in the election reached an all-time high —92.8 per cent of all eligible voters. Behind this defiant attitude, however, there was a distinct feeling of insecurity among West Berliners.

On January 10, 1959, the Soviet Union proposed the calling of a summit conference to discuss Berlin and Germany, with participation by the German Democratic Republic and the Federal Republic of Germany. Repeating its demands on Berlin, the Soviets proposed a draft peace treaty for both parts of Germany, giving each the same status. Although the six-months' deadline was not explicitly withdrawn, it was not mentioned again. Construing this as an implied retreat from duress, the Western Allies informed the Soviet government on February 16, 1959, that they were prepared to take part in a Four Power conference of Foreign Ministers to deal with the problem of Germany in all its aspects. They also consented to the presence of German advisers.

Eventually the Soviets agreed and the Foreign Ministers Conference opened in Geneva on May 11, with representatives of the two German governments present. On May 14, the Western Allies proposed a comprehensive peace plan which contained substantial concessions to accommodate Soviet interests. It was a phased plan which did not insist on immediate free elections in East Germany but provided time for a mixed German committee to draft an electoral law and work out plans for increased trade and other contacts between the two parts of Germany. Intermingled with a series of steps toward the reunification of Germany were provisions for measures against surprise attack and for progressive reductions in military forces, both in Europe and by overall ceilings on U.S. and Soviet military personnel. This far-reaching plan, which was to be implemented by stages, was designed to establish peace throughout Europe. Since it contained many concessions to the Soviet viewpoint, it was put forth as a whole to be accepted or rejected as such.

The Soviet Union instantly rejected the concessions made to it in the general plan and summarily rejected the rest of it. Further tentative concessions by the Western Allies failed to satisfy the Soviet government even as a starting point for further negotiations. As far as the Western Berlin plan was concerned, the Soviet rejection was complete and unconditional; but with the remaining parts of the Western peace plan proposals, the Soviets allowed they contained some elements which, taken one by one, could be discussed. Since the Western plan had been expressly transmitted as a related whole, the Russian evaluation was a complete rejection.

The question of Berlin was also discussed, although separately from the comprehensive plan. The Western powers took the position that if the natural solution of the Berlin question—re-establishing Berlin as the capital of a reunified Germany—could not be realized immediately, then an interim solution could be considered in which the reunification of Berlin would be a preliminary step towards the reunification of Germany. The Berlin negotiations conducted in Geneva were concerned with the preservation rather than a new status for the city.

On May 15, the Soviets submitted a counter-proposal which revolved around three major points:

1. The first was the basic Soviet contention that their occupation zone be regarded as an equal of the Federal Republic with no mention made of free elections and with no time limit on negotiations—which were to be conducted only by the two opposing German camps. Since East Germany is a puppet of the Soviet regime, this made the Soviet government practically the sole ne-

gotiator with the Federal Republic, with the Western powers completely excluded.

2. The second point involved ending the occupation of Berlin by the Western powers altogether, under the formula of establishing Berlin as a "free, demilitarized city." Since West Berlin was already a free city, the key word "demilitarized" meant the evacuation of the city by the Western Allies, leaving it defenseless and completely surrounded by Soviet controlled territory.

3. The third point laid down the withdrawal of the NATO powers from all "foreign territory" and the dismantling of all military bases. This was to be balanced by the withdrawal of Soviet forces from the Soviet Zone, Poland and Hungary.

The first point, when combined with the third, was a plan to weaken the security of West Germany and of all Free Europe, thus opening the way for the eventual extension of the communist domain. The withdrawal of military forces from and dismantling of military bases on "foreign territory" is a staple item in communist peace and disarmament proposals. This plan was a thinly disguised camouflage to expose Germany and the entire European continent to the overwhelming superiority of Soviet armed forces. It meant the expulsion of American military power from the Eurasian continent and adjacent islands and the dissolution of NATO and other alliances which restrain communist expansion by military means.

These alliances were created because of Communist threats and aggressions, notably the takeover in Czechoslovakia, the blockade of Berlin, the Communist attack in Korea, recurrent war crises in Southeast Asia, and the Soviet infiltration of Africa and the Middle East. All the alliances are defensive in character, freely entered into by their members, and in strict conformity with the United Nations Charter. It is the participation of the United States that provides the strength sufficient to deter or cope with major aggression. The presence of U.S. armed forces at various key points on and near the Eurasian continent is visible proof to friend and foe alike that the United States will honor its obligations.

In return for the withdrawal of Allied forces from West Germany and of American forces from all of Europe to the United States—some three thousand miles away—the Soviets offered to withdraw to the borders of the satellite states in the Soviet bloc—a few hundred miles away—from which they could quickly return. Certainly, this was not a peace proposal but rather a plan for conquest by making the Free nations in Europe vulnerable to Communist threats and, eventually, to outright armed aggression.

Regarding the Soviet plan for a demilitarized free city, it could not be seriously argued that the small contingents of Western Allied troops in West Berlin, which in mid-1961 numbered only 11,000, were a real threat to the peace. They were surrounded by twenty-two or more fully equipped Soviet divisions and the armed forces of the East German regime. During the more than twenty years they have been on occupation duty, Western troops have never been responsible for an international provocative incident. They remain on duty as evidence that the Western Allies will protect the freedom of West Berlin at any cost.

Since West Berlin is not a part of the Federal Republic, no West German troops are stationed there; nor has West Berlin any troops of its own. In the Soviet Zone, however, there are large numbers of well-armed East German troops on duty. During the communist May Day celebrations in 1959, 1960 and 1961, calling for the demilitarization of West Berlin, these East German forces including Russian tanks paraded ostentatiously throughout East Berlin. Such communist military displays conveyed an ominous hint of the probable fate of West Berlin if it were stripped of its military defenses by the withdrawal of its protectors. The implication became even stronger in August 1961 when large military forces, also with tanks, were deployed around East Berlin by the East German regime.

On various occasions, the Soviet authorities have suggested or hinted at certain modifications of their proposal to demilitarize West Berlin. Premier Khrushchev stated that he "would even agree to the United States, Great Britain, France and the U.S.S.R. or neutral countries maintaining some sort of minimum forces in West Berlin." He also suggested the possibility of the United Nations guarantee.

If the Russians really want the freedom of West Berlin preserved, why then do they insist on a change in the present arrangement which guarantees that freedom while preserving the peace? Khrushchev also stated that since many years have elapsed since the Nazi surrender, it is time to do away with the occupation agreements. These agreements could have been dispensed with years ago if the

Soviets had complied with them. If they had done so, or even would do so now, there would be no Berlin problem and no German problem. But the Russians still employ force not only to prevent the unification of Germany—which would automatically settle the Berlin question—but also to prohibit a free expression of will by the people of East Berlin and East Germany.

The Western powers have made it clear that they are not obligated to any particular form of protection for the freedom of West Berlin provided it does not weaken the protection which now keeps West Berlin free. Khrushchev's suggestions that this task be turned over to the United Nations should be considered in the light of his assault on United Nations' Secretary-General Dag Hammarskjold and his demand for a three-headed secretariat or "troika." Such a plan would undoubtedly paralyze the executive functions of the U.N. Secretariat.

In surmising the former Soviet Premier's real intentions regarding West Berlin, one should observe that the Soviet note of November 27, 1958, stated that "the most correct and natural" solution would be to absorb West Berlin into the German Democratic Republic. This statement was reiterated on May 30, 1959, by Soviet Foreign Minister Andrei Gromyko:

> If we are to speak frankly, the Soviet Government considers the creation of a Free City far from being an ideal solution of the West Berlin question. The most equitable approach to this question would be, of course, the extension to West Berlin of the full sovereignty of the German Democratic Republic. I think that the German Democratic Republic, whose capital the division of the city continues to mutilate, could with the fullest justification demand such a solution of the question.

The Soviet plan to make West Berlin a demilitarized free city was thus intended as a temporary expedient to "the most correct and natural solution." If Khrushchev had any doubts pertaining to the solution, his number one East German communist, Walter Ulbricht, had none. The latter's statements have the same candor as those of Hitler in "Mein Kampf."

Beginning in November 1958, Khrushchev repeatedly warned that if the Western Allies did not settle the Berlin and German questions on terms satisfactory to the Russians, he would sign a separate peace treaty with the East German regime and turn over to it the access routes to Berlin. Naturally, Moscow cannot be prevented from signing a peace treaty with any of its puppets, including East Germany. Yet this has not been done and the only conclusions can be that either the Soviets still hope to gain satellite control of all Germany without the risk of war or that they consider the risk too great to take.

The threat to peace begins with the communist contention that such a peace treaty would annul Western rights pertaining to Berlin, which is in fact contrary to international law. The threat to destroy these rights implies necessary retaliatory action to preserve them. The Western powers can accept neither the legality of the Soviet contention nor the potential consequences of such Soviet action. Free access is indispensable to the survival of West Berlin's freedom, and it is the inescapable duty of the Western powers to ensure that free access is not blocked, interrupted or whittled away. The East German regime, which under Khrushchev's plan would control all access to Berlin on the conclusion of a separate peace treaty, is a member of the Warsaw military pact of which the Soviet Union is the architect and leading member. This, then, is what made Khrushchev's declared intention a critical threat to peace and marked the second Berlin crisis.

During June 1959, the Soviet authorities called a Foreign Ministers conference in Geneva where plans proposed by both the East and the West to resolve the crisis were tabled. The conference recessed June 20, resumed July 19, and adjourned without tangible progress on August 5. It became quite apparent that the Soviet Union was not genuinely bargaining or negotiating at all but merely using the appearance of negotiation as a façade for its own determination to neutralize and demilitarize the Federal Republic of Germany. This would be a big step in breaking up NATO and taking Germany into the communist bloc.

Meanwhile, President Eisenhower invited Premier Khrushchev to visit the United States. The two leaders conferred on numerous occasions during the Russian's stay which lasted from September 15 to 27, 1959. During that period he traveled from coast to coast. Probably as a result of his visit and meetings with the President, Khrushchev suspended his threats to sign a separate peace treaty with East Germany. These and other high level conferences led to a Big Four summit meeting in Paris on May 15, 1960. All the principals were on hand and the conference about to convene when a U.S. U-2 reconnaissance plane, piloted by Francis Gary Powers, was shot down in a flight over the Soviet Union on May 1. Khrushchev refused to take part in the Paris meeting unless President Eisenhower apologized for U-2 flights over Russian territory, and the scheduled conference never took place.

The blow-up at the summit meeting, ostensibly because of the U-2 incident and the 1960 national elections in the United States, brought a pause in the talks between Washington and Moscow. Khrushchev, however, remained neither inactive nor silent, and from September 20 to October 13 he attended the United Nations General Assembly in New York. It was on one of his appearances at a General Assembly that he launched his savage attack on the Secretary-General and became the first man in the history of the United Nations to express his displeasure by taking off a shoe and pounding it on a table.

Chapter VII

Ulbricht's Communist State

East Germany plays a vital role in both the German problem as a whole and in the various Berlin crises. The Soviet Zone is composed of the pre-war German provinces of Mecklenburg, West Pomerania, Brandenburg, Thuringia, Saxony and Saxony Anholt. Exclusive of Greater Berlin, the Soviet occupied zone has an area of 41,649 square miles and a population of 16,080,374. The German people living in East Germany are also a decisive factor in whether the Soviets would risk or engage in a war over Berlin. It is pertinent, therefore, to examine the history, political background and economic conditions of these controlled areas.

As was noted earlier, the Soviet Zone does not represent the territories conquered by Russian armies during World War II. The boundaries of the occupation zones and of the Berlin area and the allocation of the zones among the Allied powers were agreed upon in September, 1944. By the night of April 13, 1945, the U.S. 83d Infantry crossed the Elbe unopposed at Barby. Fifteen miles northwest at Magdeburg, the U.S. 2d Armored Division had also crossed the Elbe but had encountered enemy opposition. On the same day, the U.S. 5th Armored Division, which had covered 200 miles in less than thirteen days, rolled into Tangermunde, just fifty-seven miles from Berlin. In one of his latest messages to Prime Minister Churchill, Supreme Allied Commander Eisenhower committed the Allied forces to rush forward and include Berlin as one of its important targets if there should be a surrender or a collapse anywhere along the front.

With bridgeheads established across the Elbe, the Supreme Commander asked General Omar Bradley what it would probably cost in casualties to move from the Elbe and capture Berlin. General Bradley estimated it might cost 100,000 American lives, and he added that that was a stiff price to pay for a prestige objective knowing that it was to be turned over to the Soviets after hostilities ceased. The U.S. troops were full of fight and eager to press forward, and their commanders were confident that Berlin would be their prize within forty-eight hours. However, the U.S. advance was halted at the Elbe on April 15 by General Eisenhower. The actual assault on Berlin was launched by two groups of Russian armies commanded by Marshals Zhukov and Koniev. Breaking through from bridgeheads on the Oder and Niesse Rivers, they easily defeated Colonel General Gotthard Heinrici's ill-equipped and ill-organized Army Group Vistula and swept into Berlin in a mopping-up type of action.

This climactic decision to permit the Soviets to take physical possession is still—twenty-two years later—a pivotal factor in communist-free world politics. If East Germany had been restricted to the territory which the Red armies actually conquered, it would be about half its present size and many of its important cities would be thriving in West Germany today.

It will be recalled that under the Potsdam Agreement, Germany was to be treated as a single economic unit under a joint Four-Power occupation, and civil liberties and democratic parties were to be encouraged. The Allied Control Commission, in accordance with the agreements made by the commanders-in-chief of the armed forces of the Four Powers on August 30, 1945, was established as the supreme organ of control in Germany during the occupation period.

During the early days of the occupation, the Soviets endeavored to convey the impression of being democratic. For example, nine of the twelve individuals appointed to head the German civil administrations in the East Zone were noncommunists. In each of these cases, however, the deputy administrator was a communist who actually functioned as the chief administrator. The same process was followed in the appointment of city mayors and their deputies. The appointment of police chiefs and police officers in the Soviet Zone was a different matter—all police chiefs and practically all police officers were communists.

During the first two months of their exclusive occupation of Berlin following the Nazi surrender, the Soviet authorities established new political parties and communist-dominated organizations. On June 10, 1945, the Soviet Military Administration authorized the organization of four political parties within the Soviet Zone and throughout Berlin as well. These parties were the Communist Party of Germany (KPD), the Social Democratic Party of Germany (SPD), the Christian Democratic Union (CDU), and the Liberal Democratic Party (LPD). These parties continued to operate after the Allied Kommandatura took over although they had no authorizations from the Kommandatura.

By November, 1945, it was apparent that the Communist Party was not achieving the anticipated success. In Austria and Hungary the Communists were badly defeated in free elections. As a result, Soviet authorities directed the merger of the Communist (KPD) and Social Democratic (SPD) Parties and a new party, the Socialist Unity Party (SED), was created early in 1946. It was recognized by the Soviets as the only authorized socialist party in East Germany. It was also recognized by the Allied Kommandatura for Berlin in May, 1946.

It is interesting to note that this forced merger was accomplished by the usual Soviet methods. The three Western Military Governments authorized the holding of a referendum in Berlin among Social Democratic Party members to determine the will of the Party by a democratic process. In the referendum, which was held on Sunday, March 31, 1946, approximately 75 per cent of the registered party members cast ballots. The result was about a nineteen to two vote against merging with the Communist KPD. However, Otto Grotewohl, the Socialist party chairman who later became the Minister-President of the Soviet Zone East German Democratic Republic, must have had some foreboding of defeat because at the last moment he ordered his party members to remain away from the polls, and he banned the referendum in the Soviet Sector.

Despite the referendum returns, the Soviets held a so-called national convention on Easter Sunday, April 21, which was attended by KPD members and selected SPD members who supported Grotewohl. Thus, the Socialist Unity Party (SED) was created and the unpopular word "Communist" was dropped from the party name. These first post-war elections, which were held in October 1946, demonstrated beyond any doubt that the communist-controlled government appointed by the Soviet authorities in 1945 was not backed by the Berliners and from that time on, the SED declined in power in all four Sectors.

The falling apart of the war alliances and the beginning of the formation of blocs in world politics were the cause of the breakdown of the joint occupation policy in Germany. By utilizing the extensive autonomous powers of the Zone Commanders under the Allied Control Council, the Soviet Union reorganized the political and economic structure of its zone of occupation on the Soviet model. The Soviets introduced radical changes into the economic life which they systematically carried out:

Agrarian reform,

The foundation of Soviet Joint Stock Companies (SAG) and People's Enterprises—nationalized businesses—(VEB),

The formation of German centralized administrative agencies in the Soviet Zone, which were replaced by the German Economic Commission in February 1948,

The over-all introduction of methods of controlled economy, and

The exclusion of Soviet zonal economy from German economy as a whole.

The formation of the SED, the "co-ordination" of the Christian Democratic Union (CDU), which supported Christian socialism as opposed to Marxian and purely materialistic theories, and the Liberal German Party (LPD) in early 1948, the build-up of communist-led mass organizations and the prevention of free elections laid the foundations of the de facto one-party dictatorship of the SED in the Soviet Zone.

Late in 1947, delegates from communist parties and mass organizations gathered for the first "German People's Congress." A second People's Congress appointed a German People's Council, composed of 300 delegates from the parties and organizations of the Soviet Zone and 100 West German representatives who were Communist Party members and fellow travelers. This Council adopted the draft of a constitution on March 19, 1948.

In order to give this People's Congress movement the outward appearance of national recognition, the third People's Congress was "elected" under a system which assured the desired allocation of the mandates in advance. Yet, even under these conditions, the proportion of invalid and negative votes polled, amounting to 38.9 per cent, demonstrated the attitude of the population so clearly that since then, no election or voting has been permitted in the Soviet Zone which would even roughly resemble the will of the people.

While the democratic system of government in West Germany was being founded on the Basic Law of May 8, 1949, the Soviet Union attempted to disguise the seizure of power by the communists in the Soviet Zone and East Berlin through a fiction of democratic legitimacy. The German People's Council, which was appointed by the third People's Congress, declared itself to be the Parliament on October 7, 1949, and implemented the "Constitution of the German Democratic Republic" by proclaiming the German Democratic Republic (GDR) on that date. Wilhelm Pieck was named president. (He was re-elected October 7, 1963 and October 7, 1957, and served until his death on September 7, 1960.) Otto Grotewohl became the minister-president (prime minister) and Walter Ulbricht was named Communist Party secretary and deputy prime minister. A Ministry of State Security, the SSD, and a militarized People's Police were organized. Pankow in the Soviet Sector of Berlin was chosen as the seat of government. Although the constitution of the GDR designated Berlin as its capital, the East Sector was not completely incorporated into the Soviet Zone. The Communists made every effort to conceal the special status of East Berlin in the new Republic, but East Berlin representatives attended meetings of the GDR Provisional Chamber of Lander (states) and the People's Chamber (Volkskammer) as observers. In actual practice, the government and the deputies of the Parliament have never been concerned with legality on a democratic basis, but have merely made a pretense of having themselves selected for office through bogus elections, the results of which are already determined in advance. The conduct of affairs lies firmly in the hands of the SED, whose official posts are reserved to communists faithful to the party line.

In 1952, the GDR Parliament abolished the five traditional provinces of East Germany as administrative units in order to eliminate a possible source of opposition from the self-administration that had been functioning. In place of them, fourteen districts of 217 counties were set up. East Berlin was considered the 15th district by the Soviets in contravention to Berlin's Four Power status. On March 26, 1954, the Soviet Union proclaimed East Germany a sovereign republic but it has kept Soviet troops there on grounds of security and the Four Power Potsdam Agreements. On September 12, 1960, after the death of Pieck, the Parliament approved a constitutional amendment that abolished the Presidency and replaced it with a new Council of State, designated as East Germany's highest governing body, with Walter Ulbricht as Chairman.

It was Ulbricht who negotiated a treaty with Poland placing Poland's boundary at the line formed by the Oder and Neisse Rivers in 1950. The United States voiced its disapproval, stating that the treaty violated the Potsdam Agreement and that no boundaries could be settled unilaterally or bilaterally outside a peace treaty. The GDR ratified an agreement with Czechoslovakia, accepting the expulsion of over 2,000,000 Germans from Sudetenland as permanent and just. It also integrated its industry with that of the Soviet Union.

There is little doubt that the leader in East Germany today, the man who follows the party line without question, is Walter Ulbricht. He was born in Leipzig, Germany, on June 30, 1893, the son of a tailor. He completed elementary school in Leipzig and became a woodworker by trade. He joined the Workers' Youth Organization at the age of fifteen and by the time he was seventeen, he was a full trade unionist in the woodworkers' union. In 1912, he became a member of the Socialist Party. He is reported to be one of the founders of the German Communist Party in 1919.

After working a few years as a Communist Party organizer in Thuringia and Saxony, Ulbricht was called to Moscow in the mid-1920's for training in the cell system of party structure. From 1928 until Hitler's rise to power in 1933, he was Communist deputy in the Reichstag of the Weimar Republic and a leader of the politburo of his party. He spent most of the years of Nazi supremacy and World War II in Czechoslovakia and Russia. He returned to Germany with Marshal Georgi K. Zhukov in 1945 as a colonel in the Russian Army. Shortly thereafter, he joined Communist Wilhelm Pieck and Socialist Otto Grotewohl in forming the SED.

Many individuals believe that he urged Premier Khrushchev to create the Berlin crises of 1958 and 1961. In his present dual position as chairman of the Council of State and first secretary of the Socialist Unity Party, Walter Ulbricht is considered the most influential German in the Soviet-controlled Zone and East Berlin.

Despite the support which the German Democratic Republic has received from Moscow and despite its external attributes of national sovereignty, it has been unable to break through the diplomatic blockade of the Western powers. Even within its own area it has not succeeded in obtaining the full support of the people. The initial circumstances under which the new Communist state was created were certainly less favorable than those which marked the founding of the German Federal Republic a short time earlier. West Germany received very substantial economic and political assistance from the Western Allies during the early stages of its life; whereas the Soviet policy of making East Germany into a separate state meant that that part of Germany, already seriously handicapped by war damage and the subsequent dismantling and removal of essential equipment and machinery, was deprived of its sources of raw materials and supplies and its connections with the industrial centers in West Germany and other parts of the free world. Furthermore, the GDR was forced to provide the Soviet Union with reparations out of its current reproduction. By the time dismantling and reparations were discontinued in 1953, their value had reached a total of approximately $11.6 billion. Many workers and businessmen fled to the West, causing a further drain of valuable economic potential. Young technicians, engineers and chemists who had been educated in GDR high schools at public expense joined in the emigration. Without this steady influx of manpower from the East, the German Federal Republic would probably have been unable to increase its economy or expand its industry at the rapid rate it achieved.

Nevertheless, in spite of these unfavorable conditions, it was possible for the communist regime in East Germany to consolidate the foundations of its economy during the period of relative political relaxation which followed the revolt of June 17, 1953. During the best years of the GDR, 1958 and 1959, the number of refugees who fled to the West diminished and, at the same time, there were more who returned to their homes in East Germany from the West. Following Khrushchev's offensive against West Berlin in November, 1958, the East German regime increased its efforts to obtain political recognition, chiefly from the non-committed states of Africa, Asia and South America. A certain amount of progress was achieved in the beginning, but it failed to develop any large degree of success because the German Federal Republic exerted considerable economic and political influence and was able to prevent the new countries from recognizing the Ulbricht regime.

During the period from 1953 to 1960, the economic gains in the East Zone should not be attributed so much to the political and economic leadership of Ulbricht's state as to the industry, resourcefulness and initiative of the East Germans. Because of these qualities and in spite of the crippling conditions of a totalitarian planned economy, a considerable increase in production was realized. Since then, there has been a serious setback in production, accompanied by lowered standards of living. This has been caused essentially by the erroneous policy of carrying the system of Bolshevism to extremes and to the general incompetence of the regime.

As an example of this ineptitude, the regime greatly overestimated its own capacity by embarking on an extremely ambitious program in the fields of aircraft construction and nuclear physics, while at the same time trying to establish a footing in neutral countries in line with the policy of granting economic assistance to developing countries, which Moscow was advocating. The policy was not only beyond the industrial capacity of East Germany, but the difficulty was aggravated by the harsh measures imposed in April 1960 for the collectivization of farms.

Under the "land reform" policies which were instituted in 1945, 11,390 farms having a total area of 6.5 million acres were appropriated. The systematic expropriation of agriculture was concluded in April 1960 with the ruthless forced collectivizaton of all independent farmers. By 1962, there were 17,860 agricultural production co-operatives with 965,000 members in the GDR. Of these cooperatives, 6,358 were operating as Type III—which means with full co-operative management and utilization of the agricultural and forest lands, cattle, machinery and implements brought into the pool by the members. From 1952 to 1962, 51,000 self-employed farmers had already fled to the German Federal Republic.

The collectivization measure jeopardized the food sources of the people on whom the regime depended. There is little doubt but that at the present time agricultural production in East Germany is one of the most difficult and dangerous problems confronting Ulbricht's government. Unless the regime is prepared to make some appreciable concessions in its farm collectivization policy, it is difficult to see how agricultural production will improve. It would appear that Ulbricht has to a large extent tied his own hands because any real relaxation of the collective farming measures might well develop into a situation beyond his control.

The entire economic structure of the Soviet Zone is still undergoing a fundamental reorganization, in the course of which most private businesses have either been forcibly nationalized or formed into co-operatives. In 1961, the share of the nationalized businesses in the gross industrial production was more than 88 per cent. Nevertheless, the SED is aware of the value of the productive output of particular branches of industry that still remain under private ownership. Instead of out-and-out dispossession, the SED is endeavoring to obtain complete control and management of the privately held portion of the economy by investing public funds in the businesses or by securing shares in private enterprises for "people-owned" undertakings. Private businesses are thereby transformed into limited companies with their former owners drawing salaries and receiving dividends corresponding to their shares of capital holdings. By 1962, 5,042 industrial enterprises, formerly privately owned, had undergone such state participation. At the end of 1961, the remaining 5,545 privately owned organizations contributed only 3.1 per cent to the gross industrial production.

Since 1957, the Soviet regime has increased its pressure on the handicraft industries which at first enjoyed a sort of exemption because of the manpower shortage. A large number of handicraft workers have added their businesses—under pressure—to the handicraft production co-operatives, thereby losing their independence. Since 1950, more than 138,000 privately owned handicraft businesses have been liquidated.

Despite the fact that the Soviet Zone is no longer required to pay any direct reparations to the Soviet Union, Moscow's policy is still one of veiled exploitation, particularly in connection with its price policy which is determined by Sovet authorities. At the present time the German Democratic Republic is the most important industrial workshop supplying the Soviet Union. From the raw materials and semi-manufactured products of Russia it produces machinery, factory equipment, ships and railroad trucks. The East Germans of the Soviet Zone have a tradition of skilled workmanship and industrial potential and by supplying manufactured goods to the relatively backward countries of the Soviet bloc and Asia, they help raise the level of production of those countries.

Notwithstanding the failures of the planned economy, the socialist buildup has been continued with Five and Seven Year Plans. According to the GDR's Statistical Yearbook, using 100 as the index, production rose in basic industry to 282 between 1950 and 1961, in the metal processing industry to 414, and in light industry to 252. It should be noted that the basis for these statistics is the index of gross industrial production caluclated by the Soviet Zonal authorities. They cannot be used in relation to the indices in international use. The 1961 exports, which were achieved at the expense of reduced consumption of goods and lowered living standards of the East Germans, were approximately 1.9 billion rubles ($2.13 billion) as compared with $12.3 billion in the Federal Republic.

The cost of living in the East Zone is at least 22 per cent higher than in West Germany. According to available statistics, in 1960 a family of four in East Germany had to spend about $109 a month to cover the cost of living in the moderate consumer group. In West Germany about $89 a month would have provided the same goods and services. For a kilogram of beef, the West German works one hour and 39 minutes; the East German, four hours and 16 minutes; for a kilogram of butter, the West German works two hours and 14 minutes; the East German, four hours and 10 minutes. The difference is even greater in the case of other items. For example, the West German works 45 minutes for a pair of ladies' perlon (German nylon) stockings; the East German, four hours and 40 minutes; for a four and one-third cubic foot refrigerator, 101 hours and 34 minutes in the West against 521 hours and 44 minutes in the East; for a television set, 304 hours and four minutes against 826 hours and five minutes. It can safely be assumed that many items of middle class living in the West are unachievable luxuries for most of the East Germans.

The Seven Year Plan (1959 to 1965 inclusive) called for an average increase in industrial production of 88 per cent. To fulfill this program and maintain the schedule required 650,000 trained university and technical school graduates by the end of 1965, and one million by 1970. According to the information provided by the East Berlin State Secretariat for University and Technical School Affairs, the planned economy needed to increase the number of students graduating from universities in 1965 from 184,000 to an estimated 337,000 in 1970; and from the technical schools from 486,000 in 1965 to an estimated 660,000 in 1970. But even the East Zone authorities appear to know that it would be impossible to train so many students in the allowable time frame.

When the central and northern regions of Germany were transformed into a Soviet satellite, with the attendant oppression of personal freedom, private ownership of business, and lowered standard of living, a drop in population resulted in those regions of almost 1,200,000 (excluding Berlin) between August 31, 1950 and December 31, 1961. During this same period, the population of the Federal Republic increased by nearly 6.2 million, the number of births over deaths accounting for nearly 3.3 million. From 1949 to 1961, over 3.6 million Germans emigrated or fled from East Berlin and the Soviet Zone to the West. Of the 1,732,282 refugees between 1954 and 1961, 863,221 were under twenty-five years of age; 6,772 were doctors; 770 were university lecturers; 17,891 were teachers; 18,871 were engineers and technicians, and 22,377 were self-employed farmers. Between 1951 and mid-1960, 21,294 members of the Soviet Zone's military and police organizations fled to the Federal Republic, and of that number, 5,058 were members of the People's Army." On the other side of the ledger, 161 members of the Federal Republic's armed forces deserted to the Soviet Zone and East Berlin. These comparative statistics are a graphic and significant indictment of communist ideology by the German people.

Nor is this the only population problem in Ulbricht's communist state. According to a special report made by the East Berlin Institute for Labor Administration, the number of births over deaths declined from 5.5 to 2.9 per 1,000 inhabitants between 1949 and 1959, and will become zero during the foreseeable future because of the lowered mortality rate due to longer length of life. The number of individuals drawing pensions per 100 able-bodied persons would have increased from 25.2 in 1955 to 34 in 1965 according to the report's estimate. At the same time, the report indicates that the number of able-bodied persons will have decreased by approximately 650,000 from 1958 to 1966.

Despite these problems, Ulbricht's communist state, with the help of the Berlin Wall, was destined to become the leading industrial country of the communist bloc next to the Soviet Union itself.

Chapter VIII

The Infamous Wall—the Third Berlin Crisis

The division of Berlin after the blockade into two unequal parts with separate and hostile political administrative and economic systems was by no means an iron curtain—at least not until August, 1961. Subways and elevated trains continued to run between both parts of the city. There was little if any hindrance to travel between the two Sectors. Though most Berliners moved their residences into that part of the city where they worked, thousands of others, called Grenzgaengers, lived in one part and worked in the other. These were mostly residents of East Berlin who had found better paying jobs in the West Sector. Friends and relatives visited each other freely and ministers preached sermons in churches in both Sectors.

During the ten-year period following the blockade, West Berliners had returned to their own private sphere of living habits and become accustomed to the rather extraordinary aspects of their life. They became inured to being unable to walk through the lake-dotted country surrounding Berlin; they got accustomed to having the VOPOS check their papers when they drove to West Germany over the Autobahn. If their papers were not in order, or if for any reason they wished to reach West Germany without advertising their change of address, those who could afford it used air travel to fly over the one hundred miles of Communist territory between West Berlin and West Germany. They also became accustomed to the presence of Allied troops in their midst and came to depend on these troops for their feeling of personal security. West Berliners accepted the fact that they were wards of the Allies and that their life was precariously balanced on the razor-sharp edge of the East-West conflict.

As the economic gap between the two Sectors increased, residents of East Berlin and the Soviet Zone went shopping in West

Berlin for goods which were not available or were of greatly inferior quality in the East Sector. Such purchases were somewhat dangerous because, in theory, they were prohibited by the communist authorities. They were also expensive because the value of the two currencies had become established at the ratio of about one West mark to four East marks; thus, the shoppers from East Berlin had to pay four times as much as the West Berliners for the same merchandise. To facilitate visits to concerts, theaters, movies and other entertainment for East Berliners and, in so doing, maintain close contact with them, West Berlin authorities adopted a plan whereby a one-to-one ratio of East to West marks was accepted for these visits. It is estimated that about a quarter of all visitors to West Berlin's movie houses came from East Berlin; 25,000 subscribers for tickets to the Volksbuenhe Theater were East Berliners; and the circuses, fairs and exhibitions depended on East Berliners' attendance for their margin of profit.

There were very few items for sale in East Berlin which were attractive to the West Berliners. However, a large number regularly patronized barbers and hairdressers in East Berlin where they had to pay only one-fourth the price charged for the same services in West Berlin. In addition, there were cultural and entertainment programs presented from time to time in the Russian Sector which drew large numbers of visitors from West Berlin.

Although travel and communication between the two parts of the divided city were permitted, a feeling of separation inevitably developed. Thousands of Germans who had entered West Berlin illegally or at one time or another had become involved in anticommunist activities felt it was dangerous to enter East Berlin. Others thought it was a needless risk since they never knew what changes of rules might suddenly occur or what might happen to them. Slowly but surely, East Berlin began to be regarded in a different light by West Berliners, and when they spoke of "Berlin" they meant West Berlin.

In the spring of 1960, Khrushchev again revived the threat of a separate peace treaty. When he scuttled the Paris Summit Conference in May, there was immediate apprehension in West Berlin that he would sign a unilateral peace treaty with the GDR and confront the Western Allies with an accomplished fact. However, on his return flight from Paris, he stopped in East Berlin and announced his intention to make no change in the Berlin situation—which he would discuss with President Eisenhower's successor.

In the second half of 1960, the Soviet Union concentrated its efforts upon West Berlin's ties with the West. The Soviets had already attempted to restrict the flight altitude of American planes in the air corridors during the previous year. They had also protested the election of the Federal President in Berlin on July 1, 1959, and tried to prevent the application of the Federal Law on Broadcasting to Berlin, which decreed that Berlin would be the location of the main offices of its board of directors. On June 30, 1960, the Soviets charged that the armed forces of the Federal Republic were being utilized in Berlin. The Western powers pointed out that the Four Power agreement was being complied with in their area in contrast to the Soviet Sector which was completely integrated into the military setup in the Soviet Zone.

The efforts of the Soviet Union to isolate Berlin from the Federal Republic in Bonn were also supported by Ulbricht through a number of measures which the Berliners called "salami tactics." The Homeland Celebration Day, which was observed in Berlin in early September, 1960, was used by Ulbricht's regime as an opportunity for turning back West German visitors to Berlin at the Zonal frontier border and for protesting civilian air transportation to Berlin, while appealing for support of Communist theories at the same time. Germans from the Federal Republic were prohibited from entering the Soviet Zone, first for a period of four days, and later for an indefinite period. On September 13, 1960, the Soviet Zone authorities refused to acknowledge passports issued to Berlin residents by the Federal Republic.

In reply to the protests from the Western Allies against these violations of the Four Power status of Berlin, the Soviet Union upheld her satellite by alleging that since the formation of two German states, German traffic in and out of Berlin was solely a matter for the Zonal regime. The Western powers pointed out that Soviet agreements with their East Zone regime did not release the Soviet Union from its obligations under the Four Power Agreement. Counter measures were promptly instituted by the Western Allies and the Federal Republic: Communist functionaries were prohibited from entering into Western countries and the international trade agreement was canceled on September 30. The latter was renewed on

December 31 with the condition of a special revocation clause in case of any obstruction to Berlin traffic. These measures resulted in a noticeable relaxation of pressure on Berlin by the Soviet Zone regime—for a time.

The Third Berlin Crisis

Early in 1961, the Soviet Union resumed its diplomatic attack against the status of Berlin by a Memorandum to the Federal Republic. The Soviets tried to make their proposal for a peace treaty acceptable to the Federal government by stressing the point that if such a peace treaty were to be concluded, the Federal Republic would be able to recommend measures favorable to itself and West Berlin at the peace conference—an opportunity which it did not have when the provisional settlement was arranged by the Four Powers prior to the end of World War II.

The first meeting between President Kennedy and Premier Khrushchev took place in Vienna on June 3 and 4, 1961. The talks were held for a direct exchange of views on Germany and Berlin without attempting negotiations and, in the word of President Kennedy, were "somber." A Soviet aide memoire on Germany and Berlin, delivered to the president on June 4, marked the formal beginning of the third great assault on the freedom of Berlin. The official translation of the aide memoire follows:

> 1. The years-long delay in arriving at a peace settlement with Germany has largely predetermined the dangerous course of events in Europe in the post-war period. The major decisions of the Allies on the eradication of militarism in Germany, which once were considered by the Governments of the United States and the U.S.S.R. as the guarantee of stable peace, have been implemented only partially and now are actually not being observed in the greater part of German territory. Of the Governments of the two German States that were formed after the war, it is only the Government of the German Democratic Republic that recognizes and adheres to those agreements. The Government of the Federal Republic of Germany openly proclaims its negative attitude to those agreements, cultivates sabre-rattling militarism and advocates the review of the German frontiers and the results of the Second World War. It tries to establish a powerful military

base for its aggressive plans, to kindle a dangerous hotbed of conflicts on German soil, and to set the former Allies in the anti-Hitler coalition against each other.

The Western Powers have allowed the Federal Republic of Germany to start accumulating armaments and setting up an army, which are clearly in excess of defense needs. The NATO Powers took new, dangerous steps when they gave the Federal Republic of Germany permission to build warships of up to 6 thousand tons displacement and also to use the territory of the United Kingdom, France and Italy for military bases of the Federal Republic of Germany.

2. The Soviet Government is earnestly striving towards removing the sources of tension between the United States and the U.S.S.R. and to proceed to constructive, friendly cooperation. The conclusion of a German peace treaty would allow the two countries to come much closer to the attainment of this goal. The U.S.S.R. and the United States fought together against Hitlerite Germany. Their common duty is to conclude a German peace treaty and thereby create a reliable guarantee that German soil will never again give birth to forces that could plunge the world into a new and even more devastating war. If the desire of the Soviet Union to consolidate peace and to prevent the unleashing of a new world war in Europe does not run counter to the intentions of the United States Government, then it will not be difficult to reach agreement.

3. Proceeding from a realistic evaluation of the situation, the Soviet Government stands for the immediate conclusion of a peace treaty with Germany. The question of a peace treaty is one that concerns the national security of the U.S.S.R. and many other States. The time has already passed for allowing the situation in Germany to remain unchanged. All the conditions for the conclusion of a peace treaty matured a long time ago and this treaty must be concluded. The point is who will conclude it and when, and whether this will entail unnecessary costs.

4. The Soviet Government is not pursuing the goal of harming the interests of the United States or other Western Powers in Europe. It does not propose to change anything either in Germany or in West Berlin in favor of any one State or group of States. The U.S.S.R. deems it necessary in the interests of consolidating peace

formally to recognize the situation which has developed in Europe after the war, to legalize and to consolidate the inviolability of the existing borders, to normalize the situation in West Berlin on the basis of reasonable consideration for the interests of all the parties concerned.

In the interests of achieving agreement on a peace treaty the Soviet Union does not insist on the immediate withdrawal of the Federal Republic of Germany from NATO. Both German States could for a certain period, even after the conclusion of a peace treaty, remain in the military alliances to which they now belong.

The Soviet proposal does not tie the conclusion of a peace treaty to the recognition of the German Democratic Republic or the Federal Republic of Germany by all the parties to this treaty. It is up to each Government to decide whether or not to recognize this or that State.

If the United States is not prepared to sign a joint peace treaty with the two German States, a peaceful settlement could be achieved on the basis of two treaties. In that case the States that participated in the anti-Hitlerite coalition would sign a peace treaty with two German States or with one German State, at their own discretion. These treaties need not be completely identical in wording but they must contain the same kind of provisions on the most important points of a peaceful settlement.

5. The conclusion of a German peace treaty would also solve the problem of normalizing the situation in West Berlin. Deprived of a stable international status, West Berlin at present is a place where the Bonn ravanchist circles continually maintain extreme tension and organize all kinds of provocations very dangerous to the cause of peace. We are duty-bound to prevent a development where intensification of West German militarism could lead to irreparable consequences due to the unsettled situation in West Berlin.

At present, the Soviet Government does not see a better way to solve the West Berlin problem than by transforming it into a demilitarized free city. The implementation of the proposal to turn West Berlin into a free city, with the interests of all parties duly taken into consideration, would normalize the situation in West Berlin. The occupation regime now being maintained has already outlived itself and has lost all connection with the purposes for which it was established, as well as with the Allied agreements concerning Germany that established the basis for its existence. The occupation rights will naturally be terminated upon the conclusion of a German peace treaty, whether it is signed with both German States or only with the German Democratic Republic, within whose territory West Berlin is located.

The position of the Soviet Government is that the free city of Berlin should have unobstructed contacts with the outside world and that its internal regulations should be determined by the freely expressed will of its population. The United States as well as other countries would naturally have every possibility to maintain and develop their relations with the free city. In short, West Berlin, as the Soviet Government sees it, should be strictly neutral. Of course, the use of Berlin as a base for provocative activities, hostile to the U.S.S.R., the G.D.R., or any other State, cannot be permitted in the future, nor can Berlin be allowed to remain a dangerous hotbed of tension and international conflicts.

The U.S.S.R. proposes that the most reliable guarantees be established against interference in the affairs of the free city on the part of any State. Token troop contingents of the United States, the United Kingdom, France and the U.S.S.R. could be stationed in West Berlin as guarantors of the free city. The U.S.S.R. would have no objections, either, to the stationing in West Berlin, for the same purpose, of military contingents from neutral States under the aegis of the U.N. The status of free city could be duly registered by the United Nations and consolidated by the authority of that international organization. The Soviet side is prepared to discuss any other measures that would guarantee the freedom and independence of West Berlin as a free demilitarized city.

All this considered, the settlement of the West Berlin problem should naturally take into account the necessity of respecting and strictly observing the sovereign rights of the German Democratic Republic, which, as is well known, has declared its readiness to adhere to such an agreement and respect it.

6. The Soviet Government proposes that a peace conference be called immediately, without delay, that a German peace treaty be concluded, and that the problem of West Berlin as a free city be solved in this way. If for any motives the Governments of the United States or other Western Powers are not ready for this at

the present time, an interim decision could be adopted for a specified period of time.

The Four Powers would appeal to the German States to come to an agreement in any form acceptable to them on problems relating to a peace settlement with Germany and its reunification. The Four Powers would declare in advance that they would recognize any agreement achieved by the Germans.

In the event of a favorable outcome of the negotiations between the G.D.R. and the F.R.G. a single German peace treaty would be agreed upon and signed. If the two German States fail to reach agreement on the above-mentioned issues, steps would be taken to conclude a peace treaty with the two German States or with one of them, at the discretion of the States concerned.

To avoid delaying a peace settlement, it is essential to fix a time limit within which the Germans should seek possible ways for agreements on problems within their internal competence. The Soviet Government considers that not more than 6 months are needed for such negotiations. This period is quite sufficient for the G.D.R. and F.R.G. to establish contacts and to negotiate, since an understanding of the necessity of putting an end to the vestiges of the Second World War in Europe has matured during the sixteen postwar years.

7. The Soviet Government is prepared to consider any constructive proposals of the United States Government on a German peace treaty and on normalizing the situation in West Berlin. The Soviet Government will show a maximum of good will in order that the question of a German peace treaty may be settled by mutual agreement between the U.S.S.R., the United States, and other States concerned. The signing of a German peace treaty by all the members of the anti-Hitlerite coalition and the settlement of the question of a neutral status for West Berlin on this basis would create better conditions for trust among States and for the solution of such important international problems as disarmament and others. But, if the United States does not show that it realizes the necessity of concluding a peace treaty, we shall deplore it because we shall be obliged to sign a peace treaty, which it would be impossible and dangerous to delay, not with all the States but only with those that wish to sign it.

The peace treaty would specifically define the status of West

Berlin as a free city and the Soviet Union, just as the other parties to the treaty, would of course observe it strictly; measures would also be taken to ensure that this status be respected by other countries as well. At the same time, this would mean putting an end to the occupation regime in West Berlin with all its implications. In particular, questions of using the means of communication by land, water or air within the territory of the G.D.R. would have to be settled solely by appropriate agreements with the G.D.R. That is but natural, since control over such means of communication is an inalienable right of every sovereign State.

8. The conclusion of a German treaty would be an important step towards the final post-war settlement in Europe for which the Soviet Union is persistently striving.

During the third Berlin crisis, the Soviet Union pursued a propaganda campaign describing the West as an aggressor if it attempted to assert its rights in Berlin against the Soviet Zone authorities. The purpose of these tactics was to convince the world in advance that the West would be responsible if any military conflict ensued. Taking advantage of the desire for peace by the people of all nations, the Soviets initiated a war of nerves over Berlin which depicted death and destruction from atomic weapons and raised the question of why 200 million people should perish in an atomic war on behalf of two million West Berliners. The West countered this policy of atomic blackmail by convincing the Soviet Union of the danger of any unilateral action and making it clear to the whole world that the Soviet Union alone was responsible for disturbing world peace.

The U.S. note of July 17, 1961, replied to the Soviet aide memoire. Similar notes were delivered the same day to the Soviet Ministry of Foreign Affairs at Moscow by the French and British Ambassadors. Pertinent excerpts from the U.S. Note are quoted:

The United States Government has given careful consideration to the Soviet Government's aide-memoire received on June 4, 1961, in Vienna. It has consulted with its British and French Allies and has found itself in full agreement with them. It has also consulted the Government of the Federal Republic of Germany, and the other member Governments of the North Atlantic Treaty Organization.

The United States Government fully concurs with the Soviet Government that a peace settlement is long overdue. It is clear from the public record of efforts on the part of the Western Powers to reach agreement with the Soviet Union on the terms of such a peace settlement that it is the Soviet Union which has blocked all progress. The United States first suggested in 1946 that a special commission be appointed to draft a German peace treaty. It has continued its efforts throughout all the intervening years but without avail because of Soviet efforts to obtain special advantages for itself and the Soviet bloc in any such settlement at the expense of a lasting peace.

The United States Government would like to be able to believe the Soviet Government's statement that it sincerely desires to remove the sources of tension between the United States and the Soviet Union and to proceed to constructive friendly co-operation. This aim is close to the hearts of the American people and their Government. It found its expression in wartime co-operation, and the United States was deeply disappointed when Soviet postwar actions disrupted the conditions for its continuation. The conclusion of a German treaty in peace and freedom and based on the freely expressed will of the German people, would, indeed, allow the U.S.S.R. and the U.S. to come much closer to the attainment of this goal.

With regard to Berlin, the United States is not insisting upon the maintenance of its legal rights because of any desire merely to perpetuate its presence there. It is insisting on, and will defend, its legal rights against attempts at unilateral abrogation because the freedom of the people of West Berlin depends upon the maintenance of those rights. The support and approval of the people of West Berlin for the system under which they live has been made amply clear over the years. . . .

The Federal Republic's foreign and military policies accepted significant restraints. It has undertaken not to manufacture atomic, chemical, and biological weapons, and has accepted international control to insure that this undertaking is honored. All of the Federal Republic's combat forces are completely integrated into NATO, which has only defensive—not aggressive—aims. The

Federal Republic does not seek, or intend to develop, an independent nuclear capability or the transfer of nuclear weapons to its national jurisdiction. It looks to its legitimate defense requirements entirely within the NATO framework. In addition, the Federal Government has publicly stated that the Federal Republic does not contemplate the use of force to achieve reunification or to alter boundaries. It has also consistently taken significant steps to integrate itself peacefully and firmly into the Western European community—steps which would never be taken by a government bent on a militaristic course.

. . . The pursuit by the U.S.S.R. of its unilateral objectives in Eastern Europe convinced the present members of NATO that Soviet power would be extended into any area westward which did not have the ability to defend itself. Should the U.S.S.R. make unilateral moves in its German policy, contrary to binding international agreements, the NATO countries could only interpret such moves as a purposeful threat to their national interests.

What the Soviet Union proposes, unless the Three Powers formally abandon their efforts to reunify Germany, is to determine by itself the fate of Germany through an agreement with the authorities of the so-called "German Democratic Republic," which is not freely chosen, but has been created by the Soviet Union as an instrument of Soviet Foreign policy.

By its signature of the United Nations Charter and in numerous statements, the Soviet Government is committed to respect for the principle of self-determination. But, in contradiction of this, by denying freedom of choice to seventeen million East Germans it has not permitted freedom of choice to the German people as a whole. And it is now proposing to perpetuate that denial by concluding a final settlement with a regime which is not representative of these people, does not enjoy their confidence, and is, in fact, no more than its own creation and an extension of its own authority. Under these circumstances, the part of Germany subject to that regime cannot be regarded as an independent sovereign state, and a "peace treaty" with the part of Germany's territory termed "German Democratic Republic" by the Soviet Government could have no validity in international law, nor could it affect in any way whatsoever the rights of the Western Powers.

According to the thesis repeatedly expounded by the Soviets, the "separate peace treaty" would, upon its conclusion, terminate the rights of the West in, and with regard to, Berlin. These assertions are untenable and fallacious from a legal point of view, both because such a separate treaty would be legally ineffective, and because neither the Soviet Union nor East Germany can, for the reasons stated above, unilaterally deprive the three Western Powers of their original rights in, and regarding, Berlin. Rights of access to Berlin are inherent in the rights of the Western Powers to be in Berlin. The procedures for the exercise of these rights have been defined in numerous agreements between the Four Governments and were confirmed by the Soviet Government in the Paris Agreement of June 20, 1949 on the termination of the Berlin blockade, and in practice over many years. They cannot be unilaterally abrogated by any act of the Soviet Government. If any one of the Four withdraws from these arrangements, then it is clearly the responsibility of the other Three to make such dispositions with respect to the exercise of their access rights as they deem appropriate.

The Soviet Union further asserts that a "peace treaty," whether signed by all the interested parties or not, would bring about the establishment of West Berlin as a "demilitarized Free City." As proposed, this would bring with it the cessation of the rights of the Western Allies in Berlin, including the right of access.

The United States considers entirely unfounded the Soviet claims that this unilateral act could deprive the other three participants in the joint occupation of Berlin of their basic rights in the City—rights derived from the Nazi surrender, as indicated, and expressed in binding and valid agreements, to which the Soviet Union is a party. The agreements of September 12, 1944 and May 1, 1945 establishing the occupation arrangements for the City were joint undertakings by the occupying powers, all of whom derived rights and obligations from them. The obligation of the Soviet Union to assure the normal functioning of transport and communication between Berlin and the western zones of Germany was reaffirmed in the Four Power Agreement of June 20, 1949. This legal situation was thus jointly created by the Four Powers and cannot be altered except by the common consent of all of them.

The United States wishes particularly to reiterate, in discussing the legal aspects of Berlin's status, that Soviet references to Berlin as being situated on the territory of the so-called "German Democratic Republic" are entirely without foundation. This can be readily and clearly established by reference to the attached copy of the Protocol of September 12, 1944. The Protocol makes clear that Berlin was not a part of, or located on, the territory to be occupied as a zone by any one of the powers under the Agreement. With respect specifically to the area now constituting the so-called "German Democratic Republic" the Protocol clearly stated that a specified area, described by metes and bounds, "will be occupied by armed forces of the U.S.S.R., with the exception of the Berlin area, for which a special system of occupation is provided below." The Protocol subsequently clearly specified that "The Berlin area . . . will be jointly occupied by armed forces of the U.S., U.K., and U.S.S.R., assigned by the respective Commanders-in-Chief." The Soviet Government approved the Protocol on February 6, 1945, and since that time there have been no legal alterations in the special status of Berlin.

The Soviet Union claims that the "free city" of West Berlin would be able to maintain freely its communications with the outside world and determine its domestic order by the free expression of the will of its people. Since, however, the "free city" would in fact be isolated within the so-called "German Democratic Republic," which according to the Soviet proposal would control all access to and from the city, it is of significance to examine the stated intentions of the leaders of that regime with respect to West Berlin.

The United States notes in particular the statements made by Mr. Ulbricht on June 15 in which he made clear his regime would seek to close Tempelhof Airport, West Berlin's principal airport and a vital part of its communications with the outside world. In addition, Mr. Ulbricht announced he "considered it a matter of course" that the refugee centers in West Berlin would be closed. These camps are maintained by West Berlin for the constant stream of refugees fleeing from East Germany, and Ulbricht's statement makes clear the degree to which his regime intends to interfere in West Berlin where it suits his purpose. In view of such statements, it is not surprising if neither the West

Berliners nor the Western Powers are reassured by professions of peaceful intent. In this connection, it is relevant to ask why the Soviet Union has chosen to raise the question at all if it has not had in mind a fundamental change in West Berlin.

It is evident that the present status of the City, which the Soviet Union chooses to characterize as an "occupation regime" constitute any threat to peace. Attempts by the Soviet Union to destroy that arrangement, in pursuit of its political goals, are certain to jeopardize gravely the very peace in the name of which the Soviet action is taken. With respect to the nature of these goals in Berlin itself, it is significant that the Soviet Union, having previously occupied East Berlin and violated its Four Power status by establishing there an alleged "G.D.R." government, now proposes that its troops will be among those stationed in a "free city" of West Berlin. The Soviet Government would thus seek to extend its post-war empire by the absorption of the Eastern sector of Berlin and to shift the Four Power principle from all of Berlin to the Western part of the city alone.

The immediate cause of this threat to peace arises from the announced intention of the Soviet Government to present the three Western Powers with a *de facto* situation based on the false assertion that they would no longer be entitled to remain in Berlin, or to have free access thereto. Such a move could lead to highly dangerous developments, and would be totally devoid of legal effect. The United States considers the exercise of its rights together with its British and French Allies, in order to maintain the freedom of over two million people in West Berlin, a fundamental political and moral obligation.

The international dispute arising out of Soviet claims would have the gravest effects upon international peace and security and endanger the lives and well-being of millions of people. It would be irresponsible on the part of the nations directly concerned not to use available means to settle such a dispute in a peaceful manner.

As in the past, the United States Government is always prepared to consider in agreement with its Allies a freely negotiated settlement of the unresolved problems of Germany. Such a settlement must be in conformity with the principle of self-determination and with the interests of all concerned. The United States Government for its part has never contemplated confronting the Soviet Union with a *fait accompli.* It hopes that for its part the Soviet Government will renounce any idea of taking such action, which, as noted, would have unforeseeable consequences. It thinks it necessary to warn the Soviet Government in all seriousness of the grave dangers of such a course, and to express the hope that the Soviet Government will rather aim, as does the United States Government, at the creation of conditions in which a genuine and peaceful settlement of outstanding problems can be pursued.

Peace and freedom are not merely words nor can they be achieved by words or promises alone. They are representative of a state of affairs.

A city does not become free merely by calling it free. For a city or a people to be free requires that they be given the opportunity without economic, political or police pressure to make their own choice and to live their own lives. The people of West Berlin today have that freedom. It is the objective of our policy for them to continue to have it.

Peace does not come automatically from a "peace treaty." There is peace in Germany today even though the situation is "abnormal." A "peace treaty" that adversely affects the lives and rights of millions will not bring peace with it. A "peace treaty" that attempts to affect adversely the solemn commitments of three great powers does not bring peace with it.

There is no reason for a crisis over Berlin. If one develops it is because the Soviet Union is attempting to invade the basic rights of others. All the world will plainly see that the misuse of such words as "peace" and "freedom" cannot conceal a threat to raise tension to the point of danger and suppress the freedom of those who now enjoy it.

In a television speech to the American people on July 25, 1961, President Kennedy made a solemn promise to defend Free Berlin and dramatically announced our new defense measures. "The immediate threat to free men is in West Berlin. But that isolated outpost is not an isolated problem. The threat is world wide." He also warned against underestimating the Western resolve to defend the Berlin rights. "We do not want to fight—but we have fought before." At the same time he declared: "We will at all times be ready to talk, if talk will help. But we must also be ready to resist with force, if force is used upon us."

It is likely that Khrushchev did not anticipate the reactions which his third assault on Berlin produced. President Kennedy recommended and the U.S. Congress promptly authorized a substantial expansion and strengthening of American armed forces. Corresponding steps were taken by other NATO members. Among these and other reactions, not the least significant was the sudden rise in the number of East Germans and East Berliners leaving the Soviet-controlled areas. In July 1961, more than 30,000 found refuge in the West—nearly twice the previous monthly average.

The East German authorities instituted new measures to stem the outward flow. They restricted travel from East Germany to East Berlin. Anyone traveling without a valid excuse was intercepted by communist control of roads and railroads. In Berlin, through more frequent checks and interrogations, they stopped and turned back some of the refugees trying to escape across the Sector border. They took steps to force some 50,000 East Berliners working in West Berlin to give up their jobs. They supported these and other harassing actions with an intensive propaganda campaign which ranged from branding refugees as traitors to inventing a polio epidemic in West Germany. They also launched a violent campaign against what they called Western "kidnapping" of the citizens of the G.D.R.

Day after day, the efforts of the East German authorities became more frantic. While they probably succeeded in blocking the flight of many thousands who were seeking freedom, they could not stop the exodus. During the first twelve days of August, more than 22,000 refugees arrived in West Berlin.

During this early part of August, the Foreign Ministers of the Western Allies were laboring feverishly in Paris, working on plans to meet all possible threats to Berlin. In the city itself, although there was an atmosphere of apprehension in the air, normal life went on and friends and relatives still visited each other across the Sector border, which was no more than a partially controlled demarcation line.

The Infamous Wall of Berlin

On Saturday night, August 12, 1961, gay crowds of East Berliners intermingled with West Berliners, window-shopping on Kurfurstendamm. Some West Berliners crossed the line to spend a convivial evening in the homes of their East Berlin neighbors. Though they did not know it, this was to be the last night of such interchange.

In the very early hours of August 13, the "little Iron Curtain" descended. Units of the People's Police, the People's Army and the factory fighting corps closed off the East Sector along its entire length by barbed wire. At 2:30 a.m., the East German authorities shut the historic Brandenburg Gate exit to West Berlin. The city was now physically divided in two. Only East Germans who had special passes were permitted to cross the border after 4:00 a.m. that Sunday morning. Most subway and elevated train service between the two Sectors was stopped though Allied military trains to and from Berlin were not affected since they were already controlled by the Russians. During the day, the number of border street crossings was reduced to 13 from the 80 which had been used during the postwar years. East German troops with armored cars and tanks were deployed along the Sector border and others were deployed on the outskirts of the city. They in turn were backed by a ring of troops from three Soviet divisions, including one tank division. Thses large-scale supporting troop organizations were obviously intended to prevent a popular uprising, such as had occurred in East Berlin and East Germany in 1953 and in Hungary in 1956, but the Ulbricht regime claimed it was carrying out a decision of the Warsaw Pact nations whose communiqué was published shortly after midnight. It was accompanied by a decree of the German Democratic Republic prohibiting all East Germans and East Berliners from entering West Berlin.

A few days later, the Communists began building an ugly wall all along the Soviet Sector boundary. This physical barrier was proclaimed as a state frontier of the German Democratic Republic. The Wall itself was constructed solidly of cement blocks, posts and barbed wire and made passage into West Berlin from East Berlin and East Germany impossible. It stopped all East German refugees immediately from fleeing into West Berlin and West Germany. As of August 23, West Berliners were forbidden to enter the East Sector and they were also warned against approaching within 100 meters of the Wall.

In various sections of the Sector boundary, the Wall runs through a purely residential area. In some of the houses and apartments,

BERLIN
0 1 2 3 4 5 km
WEST
EAST
EISKELLER
GROSSE KUHLAKE
STEINSTUCKEN
WUSTE MARK
NUTHEWIESE
June 17 Strasse
Kurfurstendamm
Friedrichstrasse
Karl Marx Allee
Havel
Müggelsee
I. Main border-crossing points authorized by Communist authorities since August 23, 1961:
1 Friedrichstrasse/Zimmerstrasse ("Checkpoint Charlie")
Only for members of Diplomatic Corps, Western Occupation Forces and non-German civilians.
2 Prinzenstrasse/Heinrich-Heinstrasse
Only for residents of Federal Republic of Germany. (West Berliners not admitted).
Also used for mail, interzonal goods and exchange of burial urns.
3 Bornholmerstrasse
Only for residents of Federal Republic of Germany. (West Berliners not admitted).
II. Minor border-crossing points (authorized by Communist authorities since August 23, 1961) for a small number of persons who are acceptable to the East Berlin authorities and who have special passes.
4 Chausseestrasse
5 Invalidenstrasse
6 Oberbaumbrücke
7 Sonnenallee
III. Additional checking points are located at Friedrichstrasse railroad station for those traveling on international trains and on the S-Bahn (elevated Interurban).
8
West Berlin's area is as large as New York City's boroughs of Manhattan, Brooklyn and Bronx combined. Since August 13, 1961 — the day the Communists built the 27 mile Wall that split Berlin in two — there have been only 8 points of intra-city crossing. Of the West Berlin enclaves shown, only Steinstücken (50 people) is inhabited.

the doorways opened on the West Sector but the interiors were entirely in the Soviet Sector. After the sealing-off measures of August 13 were begun, many people fled from their homes and residences in the Soviet Sector on to the pavements in West Berlin, leaving all their possessions behind. The People's Police immediately began bricking up the doors and windows to prevent them from returning. After many desperate East Berliners jumped from third, fourth and fifth floors and roofs into nets held by the West Berlin fire brigade, all buildings on the Soviet Sector boundary were compulsorily evacuated by the People's Police. In the fall of 1962, Soviet Sector authorities began the demolition of individual houses on the Sector border to permit better surveillance of the Wall.

Many houses and housing developments near the border were also forcibly evacuated in order to deprive the people of East Berlin of any possibility of escaping or making contact with the inhabitants of West Berlin. Closely guarded by heavily armed units of the National People's Army, evacuation commandos appeared, usually in the small hours of the morning, and forced the residents to leave within a few hours. These homeless people were temporarily accommodated in reception camps, usually school gymnasiums. Where they were finally deported to is unknown.

The construction of the Wall is not uniform. In some sections it is built of cement blocks, while other parts consist of two rows of concrete slabs supported by concrete posts, on top of which coils of barbed wire were securely attached. Including the barbed wire, the Wall stands 3.6 meters high. In front of the Wall, towards West Berlin, a two-meter high barbed wire fence has been erected. Directly behind the Wall there is a roll of barbed wire .80 meters in diameter, reinforced at numerous places by barbed-wire ties. In the middle of the roads and streets, an .80-meter high barricade of concrete posts has been installed to prevent vehicles from breaking through the Wall by force. During 1963 and '64, many sections of the original Wall were torn down and replaced with new solid concrete walls one-half to one meter thick. In March 1966, a West Berlin government spokesman estimated that building and maintaining the Wall has cost Communist East Germany about $75 million at the official rate of exchange.

In May, 1952, coincident with the entrance of the Federal Re-

(German Information Center)

From an apartment on the Soviet side of Bernauer Strasse, refugees handed their possessions to West Berliners who helped carry them across the street to freedom.

public into the European Defense Community, the East German government decreed a prohibited area on the border between the Soviet Zone and the F.R.G. Three and a half miles in depth and running 830 miles through the heart of Germany, it is very dangerous for Germans to cross in any escape attempt. Approaching the border from the Soviet side, there is first a three-mile wide off-limits strip, which may be entered only with special identification papers. Then, there is a 1,550-foot wide protective strip which is planted with beets, potatoes, and other low-lying crops. Adjoining it is a 439-foot wide security strip from which all houses, trees and shrubbery have been removed. Watchtowers have been erected on this security strip. Next, there are two barbed wire fences, one on the edge of the strip and the other 80 feet away but parallel to it. The area between the two fences is a mine field. The third barbed wire fence is an alarm equipped fence and is on the border between the two Zones. It varies from 115 to 165 feet from the second fence. The area in between has a strip of plowed land 80 to 130 feet wide and a "death strip" about 35 feet wide adjoining the alarm-equipped fence.

The most common type of barbed wire obstruction consists of three fences, three to five meters apart, each with twelve strands of barbed wire. Between the fences are one-meter high rolls of barbed wire secured with numerous cross-ties. The fences are over two meters high and are reinforced with wire entanglements.

Since August 13, 1961, 189 watchtowers have been erected in the Sector and Zonal border areas. They are 20 meters high and are equipped with searchlights and telephones. Day and night they are manned by two armed sentries from the Soviet Zonal border police. In 1962, the border police began to construct pill boxes, dugouts, rifle pits and similar means of taking cover. In some cases, these installations were camouflaged as in wartime—the underground pill box at the Spandau Zonal border, for example—or protected and reinforced by steel plates and stone walls such as at the elevated platform at Zimmerstrasse. By the end of December, 1964, 224 of these installations had been completed.

During 1963, many of the small watchtowers (up to 7 meters high) were demolished and replaced by higher and more substantial structures. The new watchtowers were frequently constructed farther back in the Soviet Zone or Sector to enable earlier detection and greater opportunity to cut off escaping refugees. Also in 1963,

(German Information Center)

The Wall is built under the watchful eyes of armed guards.

trained watchdogs were brought into specially prepared areas. The dogs are tied to 100-meter leads which permit them to range back and forth. By the end of 1964, there were 185 of these dog barricades.

The Sector and Zonal borders are guarded on the Soviet side by approximately 14,000 border police. Before August 13, 1961, and the building of the Wall, there were 6,700 border police guards. On September 15, the German police were placed under the National People's Army as a Border Detachment. Between 85 and 90 per cent of the border guards are conscripts. The border is guarded 24 hours a day by two-man sentry units which remain on duty for a straight eight-hour period. The sentry units are made up just before going on duty to prevent any collusion between guards to make their own escape. The Soviet Zonal border troops are armed with submachine guns and carry tear gas bombs and tracer ammunition.

By questioning Zonal border soldiers who have escaped and through observations of West Berlin police, it is known that border troops have instructions to prevent the flight of East Germans from the Soviet Zone and the Soviet Sector by all available means. They have orders to use their weapons and to shoot to kill after having given a warning cry or shot. If possible, they are not to shoot in the direction of West Berlin. In spite of their instructions, there are numerous cases where refugees have been fired upon with intent to kill without a warning cry or shot having been given. According to reliable information, the border soldiers involved were not called to account but were decorated and given bonuses instead.

Prior to August 13, refugees from the Soviet Sector or Soviet Zone could go to West Berlin via the elevated or underground railways which covered all of Berlin. Although the People's Police or the Transport Police took various measures to prevent travel by refugees, this escape route was nevertheless relatively without danger and therefore the one most frequently used. The sealing off of the Soviet Sector from West Berlin, which began on August 13, made escape from the Communist orbit incredibly difficult and dangerous. Many persons paid for their escape attempts with their lives; others were arrested and sentenced to long terms of penal servitude. To overcome the barricades to freedom, the refugees escaped by numerous special routes and ingenious ruses. Some of the methods

(German Information Center)

Police dog patrols the Wall which divides Berlin at a cemetery.

used, the disclosure of which will endanger no one or prevent future escape opportunities, may be described.

In the beginning, refugees leaped from windows and roofs of buildings along the border into nets of the West Berlin fire brigade, as mentioned earlier. This method no longer is available since all buildings on the border have been evacuated and walled up or demolished.

Many persons reached West Berlin through underground sewers. This route has been blocked with grates put over the sewers and electric warning systems have been installed.

Some refugees swam across the border. On January 1, 1963, a young woman swam across a border canal near the Upper Freiarch Bridge when the temperature was twelve degrees below zero centigrade (about 12° above F). This method has become even more hazardous since underwater barbed wire obstructions have been laid. Many refugees have been fired on and some killed while swimming across the border boundary.

Clever and desperate ruses have also been used to reach West Berlin. A number of refugees deceived the guards by wearing self-made uniforms. Two families with eleven children were hidden by the driver under a load of frozen meat in a refrigerator truck. In another instance, a workman reached West Berlin by clambering across a disconnected high-tension cable.

Many escapes were made by tunnels under the Wall. In January 1962, 28 persons, between the ages of eight and seventy-one, reached West Berlin by crawling through a tunnel they had laboriously dug themselves. In September 1962, 29 persons escaped through a tunnel which had been dug from West Berlin. In May 1963, after fourteen days of tunneling, 12 persons escaped to the West. Early in October 1964, 57 persons escaped through a tunnel 140 meters long, which was completed after months of work by 36 West Berliners. The difficulties of secretly carrying on such complicated engineering projects by the unskilled, with only the tools they could find easily available, the cave-ins, alarms and fearsome labor were graphically dramatized in a television presentation not soon to be forgotten by those who saw it.

Some escapes were made by breaking through the barricades by force. In December, 1961, 25 escapees from the Soviet Zone seized the local train from Oranienburg to Albrechtshof, ran it through the border barricades and reached Spandau. In June 1962, 14 residents of East Berlin escaped to West Berlin by taking over an excursion steamer lying at anchor in the Soviet Sector. The following April, a mechanic rammed an armored truck of the People's Army through the wall at Elsenstrasse and escaped, although he was severely wounded by Zonal border guards.

Some refugees have escaped by roundabout routes through foreign countries. Some sailed as passengers or crew on Soviet ships and jumped ship in ports of the free world. During the Communist World Youth Festival in Helsinki in August 1962, 41 members of the Soviet Zone delegation managed to escape despite being closely guarded.

The point that only misery and desperation and a true love of freedom can drive men, women and their families to take such fantastic risks to escape from Communism does not need to be belabored.

Reaction of the Western Allies to the Wall

The barricading of the frontier on August 13 was considered by the Western Allies to be a flagrant and particularly serious violaton of the quadripartite status of Berlin and drew immediate protests. The following is the text of the protest letter from the three Western Commandants to the Soviet Commandant on August 15, 1961:

> During the night of August 12-13 the East German authorities put into effect illegal measures designed to turn the boundaries between the West sectors of Berlin and the Soviet sector into an arbitrary barrier to movement of German citizens resident in East Berlin and East Germany.
>
> Not since the imposition of the Berlin blockade has there been such a flagrant violation of the Four-Power agreements concerning Berlin. The agreement of June 20, 1949, in which the U.S.S.R. pledged itself to facilitate freedom of movement within Berlin and between Berlin and the rest of Germany, has also been violated.
>
> In disregard of these arrangements and of the wishes of the population of this city, for the welfare of which the Four Powers are jointly responsible, freedom of circulation throughout Berlin has been severely curtailed. Traffic between the East sector and the Western sectors of Berlin has been disrupted by the cutting of S-Bahn and U-Bahn service, the tearing up of streets, the erection

of road blocks, and the stringing of barbed wire. In carrying out these illegal actions, military and paramilitary units, which were formed in violation of Four-Power agreements and whose very presence in East Berlin is illegal, turned the Soviet sector of Berlin into an armed camp.

Moreover, the East German authorities have now prohibited the many inhabitants of East Berlin and East Germany who were employed in West Berlin from continuing to pursue their occupations in West Berlin. They have thus denied to the working population under their control the elementary right of free choice of place of employment.

It is obvious that the East German authorities have taken these repressive measures because the people under their control, deeply perturbed by the threats on Berlin recently launched by Communist leaders, were fleeing in large numbers to the West.

We must protest against the illegal measures introduced on August 13 and hold you responsible for the carrying out of the relevant agreements.

On August 17, the United States government protested the closure of the Soviet Sector in a Note to the Soviet Government:

The Embassy of the United States presents its compliments to the Minister of Foreign Affairs and upon instructions of its Government has the honor to direct the most serious attention of the Government of the U.S.S.R. to the following.

On August 13, East German authorities put into effect several measures regulating movement at the boundary of the western sectors and the Soviet sector of the City of Berlin. These measures have the effect of limiting, to a degree approaching complete prohibition, passage from the Soviet sector to the western sectors of the city. These measures were accompanied by the closing of the Sector boundary by a sizable deployment of police forces and by military detachments brought into Berlin for this purpose.

All this is a flagrant, and particularly serious, violation of the quadripartite status of Berlin. Freedom of movement with respect to Berlin was reaffirmed by the quadripartite agreement of New York on May 4, 1949, and by the decision taken at Paris on

June 20, 1949, by the Council of Ministers of Foreign Affairs of the Four Powers. The United States Government has never accepted that limitations can be imposed on freedom of movement within Berlin. The boundary between the Soviet sector and the western sectors of Berlin is not a state frontier. The United States Government considers that the measures which the East German authorities have taken are illegal. It reiterates that it does not accept the pretension that the Soviet sector of Berlin forms a part of the so-called "German Democratic Republic" and that Berlin is situated on its territory. Such a pretension is in itself a violation of the solemnly pledged word of the U.S.S.R. in the agreement on the zones of occupation in Germany and the administration of Greater Berlin. Moreover, the United States Government cannot admit the right of the East German authorities to authorize their armed forces to enter the Soviet sector of Berlin.

By the very admission of the East German authorities, the measures which have just been taken are motivated by the fact that an ever increasing number of inhabitants of East Germany wish to leave this territory. The reasons for this exodus are known. They are simply the internal difficulties in East Germany.

To judge by the terms of a declaration of the Warsaw Pact powers published on August 13, the measures in question are supposed to have been recommended to the East German authorities by those powers. The United States Government notes that the powers which associated themselves with the U.S.S.R. by signing the Warsaw Pact are thus intervening in a domain in which they have no competence.

It is to be noted that this declaration states that the measures taken by the East German authorities are "in the interests of the German peoples themselves." It is difficult to see any basis for this statement, or to understand why it should be for the members of the Warsaw Pact to decide what are the interests of the German people. It is evident that no Germans, particularly those whose freedom is being forcibly restrained, think this is so. This would become abundantly clear if all Germans were allowed a free choice and the principle of self-determination were also applied in the Soviet sector of Berlin and in East Germany.

The United States Government solemnly protests against the measures referred to above, for which it holds the Soviet Govern-

(German Information Center)

Berlin Wall: Crossing point into East Berlin.

ment responsible. The United States Government expects the Soviet Government to put an end to these illegal measures. This unilateral infringement of the quadripartite status of Berlin can only increase existing tensions and dangers.

The Soviet Union replied to the protests of the Western Military Commandants and of the American, British and French governments with statements in which they said they were only denying to the West the right to interfere in the internal affairs of the German Democratic Republic, which had merely made use of the rights common to every sovereign state to protect its interests. The Soviets demanded that the Western powers accept this view and normalize the situation in West Berlin through the conclusion of a peace treaty.

On August 19, with the Sector border almost completely sealed, U.S. Vice President Lyndon B. Johnson, former U.S. Ambassador to Moscow Charles E. Bohlen, and former U.S. Berlin Commandant General Lucius D. Clay arrived in Berlin to reassure West Berliners that the United States would stand by its pledges to defend the freedom of West Berlin and its access routes. The following day, a U.S. combat unit of 1,500 men arrived to reinforce the American garrison in West Berlin. The convoy traveled the 110 miles from Mannheim to Berlin along the Helmstedt-Berlin Autobahn and passed through all Soviet checkpoints without incident.

On August 23, the Ministerial Council of the German Democratic Republic called upon all persons, in the interests of their own safety, to stay 100 meters away from both sides of the border between East and West Berlin. The three Western Commandants lodged a sharply worded protest against this new encroachment. They also moved combat troops with heavy tanks and armored cars to positions along the border, and armored cars were used to maintain continuous patrols along Sector and Zonal borders of West Berlin. The number of West Berlin police on duty to guard against intrusions on the Sector and Zonal borders was increased fivefold and, for the first time, they were armed with rifles and submachine guns. Helmeted U.S. soldiers moved their tanks into the 100-meter "forbidden" area so that the barrels of their tank guns pointed directly over the Communist barricades. At a press conference on August 30, President Kennedy announced that General Lucius D. Clay was returning to Berlin as his personal representative.

The restricted local counter measures taken by the Western Allies clearly showed that they insisted upon both their rights and obligations in West Berlin and their right of free access to their portion of the city. In August, 1961, the Soviet Union again initiated new steps of harassment against non-military flights to Berlin. The Western powers maintained that their unrestricted right to free access also included German traffic with Berlin and they emphatically repeated their warning that they would regard any obstruction of flights to Berlin as an attack upon themselves.

Thus, the international situation continued to be strained and a peaceful settlement of the German problem became more remote than ever.

Chapter IX

Impact of the Wall on Berlin

Behind the Wall

Ulbricht and his puppet government were given a certain amount of encouragement by the annexation of East Berlin which resulted from the erection of the Wall. It also provided a unilateral solution to the painful and urgent problem of stopping the mass flight of refugees to the West. The *de facto* acceptance by the Western Allies of the sealing off of East Berlin was celebrated by the East German communist leaders who ordered the flag of the German Democratic Republic to be flown on a ten-meter high flagpole on the Brandenburg Gate. Ulbricht announced at that time that it would be his state that would direct the course of German history in the future.

From the fall of 1958 to the building of the Wall, East German authorities had been able to crush every form of opposition within their own sphere by directing attention to the separate peace treaty which was supposed to be impending and to the consequential elimination of the Western powers in West Berlin. In the spring of 1959 they were so confident of victory that they were singing "When the lilac blooms again, we'll dispose of West Berlin," referring to Khrushchev's six months' ultimatum. However, because of steadily increasing economic difficulties and the unredeemed Communist Party promises on the Berlin question, Ulbricht's functionaries were forced more and more on to the defensive. Today, none of the official statements of the Communist Party contain any specific reference to the separate peace treaty or to future Soviet policies on the Berlin problem. It would appear that, at least for the time being, the Communists are resigned to the failure of their offensive again West Berlin.

It would be a great mistake, however, to underestimate the significance of the Wall in the long-term prospects for the G.D.R. East Berlin does not legally belong to the G.D.R. but, as previously noted, it is a part of Greater Berlin, which was agreed upon by the Four Powers in the closing stages of World War II and put into effect by them after the war. Its annexation closed the last gap in the barbed wire fence stretching from Lubeck in the north to Hof in the south. It made it possible for Ulbricht to disregard the feelings of the imprisoned Germans and put his program of Bolshevism into effect. It also enabled him to make a reasonably accurate estimate of his future labor potential, which up to August 13 was not possible.

When freedom of travel between the East and West Sectors of Berlin was guaranteed by the Four-Power status of the city, residents of the Soviet Zone and East Berlin could escape from communist oppression by fleeing to the West. In those times many thousands of East Berliners were daily visitors in West Berlin in addition to those who traveled to the city to earn their living. As a result, the moral and spiritual influence of West Berlin on the G.D.R. was significant. Because of the Wall, West Berlin is no longer a meeting-place for East and West German residents. Consequently, it has lost some of its ability to influence Eastern Germany—thus affording considerable relief to Ulbricht's regime.

The individuals who were hardest hit by the Wall were the intellectuals in East Berlin and the Soviet Zone. Formerly, with the ever-present opportunity to flee to the West, they occupied a privileged position in comparison with similar groups in other satellite states of the Eastern bloc. If the communist regime pressed them too hard, they could threaten to emigrate. Since the Wall, Ulbricht has adopted a tougher attitude with the intellectuals. He is no longer satisfied with lip service to the cause of socialist reconstruction but, instead, he insists that they actively cooperate in educating the young people to become Communists, prepared to take part in the class struggle.

The erection of the Wall has not solved all or even many of the most important problems confronting the G.D.R. The longer this concrete monstrosity exists, the greater will be the desire of those Germans who have been cut off from the West to share in the many activities, friendly lights and freedom of West Berlin. They will long for the opportunity to engage in intellectual discussion without fear or compulsion, for the chance to meet friends and relatives from the West, and for shopping in the well-stocked stores which private enterprise has created. It is small wonder that editorials in a Soviet Sector newspaper appealed to its readers to pay attention to the Soviet achievements of today in East Berlin instead of gazing at the flood-lighted façade of the Berlin Hilton Hotel.

It has often been said that Ulbricht complains that the young painters in the G.D.R. use too much gray coloring in their pictures, that sculptors and graphic artists create figures which do not inspire hope, and that the "first workers' and peasants' state" lacks fresh, optimistic faith in the future. A young Communist woman author is reported to have written that the youth who had been brought up according to Stalin's ideas, and who had once believed that a new order could be discerned rising above the horizon, had now succumbed to the weariness and cynicism of angry young men. In discussions with visitors from the West, many Communists of long standing admit that they cannot understand the young people of East Germany who learn to repeat the Marx-Leninist doctrine by heart without believing it, and all the time are only acting a part. Certainly this condition in the G.D.R. cannot be attributed to the building of the Wall, but it has doubtless been accentuated by the continued existence of the Wall.

The farmers, who were forced to enter the agricultural collectives, constitute a fairly coherent group which is opposed to the regime. They submitted to the agrarian "reforms" not because they were capitulating to the regime, but because they wanted to survive with as little damage as possible from the farm collectivization program, and they looked forward to the day when they could return to their normal farming customs. Ulbricht's farm program was probably instituted under the assumption that the Soviet Union would soon resolve the Berlin problem according to its wishes. The passage of time has proven this to be a mistake; and, in view of the stalemate in the East-West struggle and the continued presence of the Western Allies in West Berlin, in the heart of the Soviet Zone, the farmers refuse to abandon hope for the future.

The industrial workers are another group who still retain their hope for freedom. They possess a trade union tradition of which they are justly proud and, so far, the Communist Party has been unsuccessful in replacing the old Social Democrat and trade union ideas with Communist and totalitarian ones.

While Ulbricht's psychological position is practically the same as it was in 1953, his communist state is enjoying the nearest thing to a boom yet seen in the communist world. The standard of living in East Germany is the highest of any Soviet satellite. With a population of 17 million (United Nations, 1964 estimate), the Soviet Zone stands as the tenth largest industrial producer in the entire world. This was accomplished without Marshall Plan aid or assistance from satellite countries and in spite of the stripping and dismantling of East German factories during the first eight to ten years after the war. This latter measure has resulted in an unforeseen and unintended benefit—by replacing the equipment taken by the Soviets with new equipment, East Germany now possesses new and relatively modern industrial facilities. As an example, half the machinery in the top-priority chemical industry is less than ten years old.

Most of East Germany's foreign trade is with other communist countries. Soviet government policy limits commerce with Western nations to approximately one-fourth of East Germany's total trade, which amounted to about $1.5 billion out of $6 billion in 1965. Ten per cent of the foreign trade with the Free World is with West Germany. While its hard currency position could be improved by increasing trade with West Germany, a trade embargo would undoubtedly be put into effect in the event of another Berlin crisis. Then, if other Western nations joined the embargo, the economy of East Germany would be seriously affected.

Since 1949, only about 900,000 housing units have been built in East Germany. Individual houses are built only for top Communist bureaucrats. Other residents live in large apartment buildings, most of which are poorly constructed and drably painted. After a few years, they look more like factories than apartments. Rents, however, are low, running from about $10 to $12 a month for a small unit to $35 a month for a five-room apartment in the upper class. Small two-room apartments can be purchased in cooperative buildings for as little as $1,000.

Bargains in housing are partially offset by the cost of food: butter—which is rationed a half pound per individual every ten days—costs $1.25 per pound; coffee varies from $7.50 to $10 per pound, and a 3-ounce chocolate bar costs $1.20.

Automobile prices are so high that only about one person in twenty-five can own a car. Motorcycles and bicycles are still the principal means of private transportation for most East Germans.

(German Information Center)

Street scene in East Berlin—the "Workers Paradise"

Midget cars cost about $2,000 apiece, while larger cars cost from $3,500 to $4,500—and they are also small by American standards. Gasoline is high, costing about $1.40 a gallon. With the average worker being paid $35 a week, it is obvious that the communist authorities are not anxious to enable East Germans to own and drive cars.

On the other hand, communism has brought high living to one group of East Germans. This group includes not only the senior members of the Communist Party, but also leaders in literature and the arts, teachers, lecturers, professors, technical specialists, and other intellectuals who serve the communist regime. These favored ones receive special privileges such as individual homes, and drawing accounts for the purchase of television sets, refrigerators and Western-made automobiles. When traveling, they are not subject to the normal currency control restrictions and are able to enjoy vacations at luxury resorts in communist countries.

In general, however, East Germans have become resigned to accepting life under communism—whether they like it or not. Since the erection of the Wall, opponents of the regime realize there is no escape if they get into trouble. At the same time, the East Germans have developed an attitude of significant independence toward the Russians. Only communist publications are permitted to enter East Germany but the regime has given up trying to jam radio and TV programs, which are picked up from West Berlin stations. As stated earlier, one of the biggest communist concerns is the failure to win East German youth to communism after more than twenty years of iron rule.

More than twenty divisions of Russian troops are stationed in East Germany, and it would appear likely that without these troops, Ulbricht's regime would fall. The rebellion of 1953 has not been forgotten, so it is just as likely that Russian troops will continue to remain in East Germany.

In West Berlin

The construction of the Wall was a tremendous shock to West Berliners and the absence of a forceful response by the Western Allies caused many to wonder whether the United States would stand behind its guarantees if the Communists proceeded further. Most West Berliners entertained the doubt that Berlin was worth the risk of all-out war to the Allies. Convinced that the only language the Soviets understand is that of force, any appearance of weakness by the Western Allies—such as permitting Ulbricht's regime to cut off free communication in Berlin unhindered—was viewed as leading to further aggressive measures which would climax eventually in the total conquest of the West Sector. West Berliners, deeply shaken by the communists' open show of military force, were not prepared to accept the distinction between Allied rights in West Berlin as contrasted to those in East Berlin. The fact that the gradual annexation of East Berlin into the communist sphere of authority had been progressing for more than a decade, and that the Western powers had never forcefully attempted to stop this development, was generally overlooked. To the West Berliners, the Wall was another serious defeat for the West.

The apprehension of the West Sector residents concerning U.S. guarantees of West Berlin was of short duration. Vice President Johnson and General Clay arrived in Berlin on August 19, and a U.S. combat unit arrived on August 20 to reinforce the American garrison. Both events received an enthusiastic welcome. It was the first concrete sign that the United States was not abandoning West Berlin and it was a great relief to the population. Their awareness that the arrival of the statesmen and troops was no effective counter measure designed to restore Berlin to its pre-August 13 status did not dampen their ardent reception. They were satisfied that, at least for the time being, West Berlin was safe from Russian troops.

Apart from those individuals who suffered great personal sadness and tragedy through enforced separation from friends and family, the Wall had a profound impact on the life of West Berlin. To begin with, it stopped the 50,000 East German boundary commuters from coming in daily to work in West Berlin. Some of them were forced by the Soviet regime to perform hard labor in the mines as punishment for their long years of completely legal employment in their hereditary Berlin firms. West Berliners also missed other helping hands: the thousands of girls and women who also came over every day to look after children, clean apartments and help out in over-worked offices and under-staffed stores. The Wall also ended the flow of refugees who were necessary to maintain West Berlin's population level against loss from deaths and migration to the West.

(German Information Center)

West Berlin street sign facing the Wall: "Unity and Justice and Freedom" (from the German national anthem).

The city was deprived of its functions as the show window of the Free World and as a haven for refugees. Further, the Wall emphasized the abnormal situation of West Berlin as an island in the midst of the Soviet Zone and tended to reopen the question concerning the city's long-range future.

Since August 13, the morale of the population has become a decisive factor in the future of West Berlin. The people of all West Germany received a tremendous lift in spirits when President Kennedy visited the city in June 1963 and declared: "All free men, wherever they may be, are citizens of Berlin. Therefore, as a free man, I take pride in the words: 'Ich bin ein Berliner!' "

The present situation differs materially in its demands on the city's inhabitants from that of the blockade period when they were confronted with what was primarily a combat situation of limited duration. Then, what was required of each West Berliner to meet the crisis was clear-cut. The threat and the visible Allied response built solidarity among the people and strengthened the bonds of confidence and understanding between the people and the Allied armed forces. Today, there is no end in sight to the threat and the West Berliner is not certain what is expected of him. Moreover, the very indefiniteness of the crisis tends to become extremely wearisome after a while.

With its improved standard of living over its 1948-49 level, and the integration of its economy with that of West Germany, the city has become more rather than less vulnerable to crisis. Whereas it existed at an artificially maintained subsistence level during the blockade, now it is part of an economic system in which viability depends on the preference of the residents to pursue their work in West Berlin rather than to move to some other more tension-free community. Under such conditions, there is little to be gained by appealing to the population for service in and duty to their city. Such an action might present West Berlin as a symbol of a front line city in the East-West struggle and frighten away the very people it wished to reassure. Nevertheless, the interest of the Western Allies and the West German government in the fate of Berlin must be maintained, and this can only be done by reiterating its role in the Cold War and its division by the Wall.

How do West Berliners normalize their everyday life without forgetting the hardships of their fellow countrymen behind the Wall

(German Information Center)

Typical week-day scene on Kurfurstendamm, showing the ruins of the original Kaiser Wilhelm Memorial Church and the modern construction of the new Memorial Church.

or without becoming immune to its existence? In the struggle between normalcy and the crisis created by the Wall, stabilizing forces have been gaining ground and tensions have been lessening. West Berliners are being encouraged by their political leaders to believe in the future, and to work and raise a family. Visitors, workers and businessmen are being attracted to West Berlin because it is a bright, growing city where one can live pleasantly and earn a good living. West Berlin authorities have been actively developing plans to assure the future of the city. One prerequisite for the realization of such plans is physical security against Communist aggression. This is guaranteed by the presence of armed forces of the Western Allies in West Berlin. Another requirement is the maintenance of at least one access route entirely free of communist control—as the air corridors currently provide—so that no one need fear traveling in and out of the city.

In addition, an atmosphere of confidence is necessary to keep those living in West Berlin from leaving and to attract new people to it from the West. This is most easily accomplished in the business field because it is possible to make capital investment in West Berlin more profitable and less risky than in other parts of Germany. The expansion of West Berlin's economic capacity and the establishment of new enterprises in the city are supported by a variety of special measures. These include investment credits provided by European Recovery Program Special Funds and other loans for business investments available through the Berlin Industrial Bank.

Within the framework of the law, the Federal Republic of Germany guarantees loans for capital equipment investment as well as other business investments, provides loans for the construction of housing, factories and office buildings, accepts liability for all goods moving in and out of West Berlin, provides reduced rates for postage and air transport, provides preferential treatment with respect to turnover, corporation and income taxes, and allows for the write-off of certain investments.

It is difficult, however, to persuade working-age people to move to West Berlin from West Germany as long as there is full employment in the national economy. Special inducements, such as exceptionally low interest rate loans for newly married couples and a special housing program for newly arrived workers, are being offered. In addition, traveling and moving expenses of new workers to West

Berlin are reimbursed. If the worker settles in West Berlin with his family, or marries and stays in West Berlin, he is entitled to a family foundation loan. This free loan has a maturity of eleven years and for any child born during that time, the loan will be reduced by 25 per cent.

However, West Berlin employers cannot be expected to pay wages above the average level prevailing in West Germany, and the possibility of subsidizing wages with government funds is extremely limited. It is only natural that as long as the economy of West Germany remains prosperous, its freedom of travel will make it more attractive than the necessarily restricted conditions in West Berlin.

Of particular interest is the widely discussed plan to create a large-scale center of culture and learning in West Berlin to attract students, scholars and artists to the city in large numbers. It is envisaged as the intellectual capital of Germany, even though it cannot be the political capital. Funds are being expended to enlarge the existing universities and to establish additional scientific institutions and teachers' colleges. It is still an open question whether the large expenditure of funds in cultural and scientific institutions will accomplish the desired result. Nevertheless, the Free University, which opened for its first term with 2,140 students on December 4, 1948, during the blockade, now has 14,000 students from all over the world on the campus of eighty university buildings in the suburb of Dahlem. West Berlin also has many other educational and cultural institutions: the Technical University, the Conservatory for Music, the School of Fine Arts (for painters, artists and sculptors), a professional high-level school for typography and advertising, and several trade schools and research centers.

One of the little publicized activities conducted by the authorities of East and West Germany concerns the ransoming of prisoners held by East Germany. Take the case of two young Germans, a 20-year-old truck driver and his friend, a 21-year-old machinist, who decided to crash the Heinrich-Heine-Strasse checkpoint one summer night in a stolen truck. Intercepted by East German police before they reached the border, one drew a two-year sentence in Bautzen Labor Camp and the other a twenty months' sentence in Buetzow Prison. Some months later, they were suddenly removed from their cells, driven to a West German crossing point and turned loose.

These two young men became members of a select group of some 2,200 East German prisoners who have been ransomed from the Soviet Zone in the last few years. Arrangements for the release of such prisoners are made by West German lawyers with the approval of the Minister of All-German Affairs of the Bonn government. They are financed by the Federal government and West German industrial firms which receive an appropriate tax reduction. It is reported that so far the cost has been about $24 million. No money changes hands, however. Ulbricht's communist regime takes payment in West German luxury consumer goods—coffee, butter, citrus fruits, trucks and spare parts. Young Germans, such as those referred to, are needed to fill the labor shortage in West Berlin and can be ransomed for about $4,000 each. Those convicted of sabotage, espionage and subversion by the Communists bring about $10,000 each.

The Bonn government has clamped a tight lid of secrecy on these barter arrangements, probably fearing that if it were common knowledge it might prove embarrassing to the East German regime, who would then terminate it. At the same time, West German authorities, in scrupulous observance of the law, have handed out stiff penalties to West Germans who help East Berliners escape. U.S. newspapers reported in February, 1966, that three West Germans who aided East Germans dressed in U.S. military uniforms to pass across the border received jail sentences from West German courts, and two American soldiers involved were demoted and given hard labor sentences.

It cannot be stated with any certainty whether the Wall has strengthened or weakened the spirit of the West Berliners. Since it was not followed by other communist military offensive actions, it may have re-inforced the feeling of the population that having been through so much, they can cope with whatever else may come up. Being realists, the majority of West Berliners know that, at least for the foreseeable future, they will have to live with this monstrous creation. Yet, they must never cease to cry out against it and to hope that some day, somehow, the infamous Wall must come down.

Chapter X

Military-Political Aspects

If West Berlin is not vital to the Soviet Union from purely material or geographical considerations, what is the aim of the Soviet government in repeatedly assaulting it? Why are the Soviets endeavoring to impose their own radical solution on the Berlin problem?

From the Soviet government's point of view, the question of Berlin's status is an immediate issue but not the real issue. It is only one step in the Communist plan for world-wide domination. Until August 13, 1961, West Berlin was a showcase for Western technology and an escape channel for millions of inhabitants of the East Sector and Eastern Zone. Today, West Berlin is a lonely lighthouse of freedom in a dark totalitarian sea. It demonstrates the material superiority of a free society which allows and encourages individual initiative—also, it is a model of political, intellectual and spiritual freedom in which individual liberties are assured and the people are free to choose those who govern them. Thus, West Berlin is a constant irritation and embarrassment to the Soviet regime, both in Germany and in Russia.

The East Zone authorities function under the direction of the Soviet Union which has shown little interest in the welfare of the German people living in Ulbricht's barbed wire paradise. One of the reasons why the control of the Soviet Zonal regime has had to depend on Soviet troops is that East Germany has been so greatly exploited politically and economically by the Soviet government. The Zonal leaders have had to carry out and enforce the Soviet government's directives from production and distribution to overt propaganda—measures which related solely to the problems of the Soviet Union.

Khrushchev was relentless in exploiting Berlin's status as a means of securing recognition for Ulbricht's regime from the Western powers. This indicates the long-range Soviet strategy with respect to Berlin and the German problem. The Soviet aim is to disrupt NATO and the European Community, using Berlin as a means of accomplishing these objectives. NATO's current difficulties with France cannot be attributed to the Soviet regime, but it is obvious that the Communists are not displeased with the turn of events.

The Federal Republic with its economic prosperity, a popular dislike for Communism and a practically nonexistent Communist Party, is not a fertile field for Soviet propaganda. The first step in the Soviet program is, therefore, to create a mood of discouragement and disenchantment in the Federal Republic with the results of its adherence to NATO and the European Community. Efforts are also being made to engender mutual distrust among the Western Allies and exploit their differences.

The potentialities inherent in the integration of West European nations are tremendous and the Soviet Union has been forced to accept it as a distinct possibility. With full integration, the Western countries of Europe would be united in an organization whose technological and military potential would exceed that of the Soviet Union. Any hopes entertained for an advance westward into Europe would then be futile and on a world-wide scale, the Soviet Union might be relegated to be a third-rate power.

Without the Federal Republic, European integration would not be possible and therefore the Federal Republic has become the primary target of Soviet political maneuvers in Berlin. The first phase of the Soviet strategy is to attempt to disillusion the Federal Republic about its success with Western policies. The psychological weakening of Bonn's support for NATO, the European Community and other Western organizations would sabotage the entire Western undertaking. This point is probably not lost on the Kremlin leaders.

The Soviet determination to induce the West to recognize the Soviet Zone as a state is based on the fact that such recognition could postpone indefinitely the reunification of Germany. In actuality, it might make it an historical impossibility. The Western powers pledged themselves to support a policy of ultimate reunification and never to recognize two German states in the Paris Treaties of 1954. Therefore, the Soviets may consider that if the West would abandon a position taken so unequivocally years ago, it could cause an agonizing reappraisal of policy within the Federal Republic, and the first step in the Soviet program would be achieved.

Actually, what the West is being asked to acknowledge in Berlin is an agreement with the Russians to partition all of Germany into three separate parts: the Federal Republic, the Soviet Zone, and the "Free City" of West Berlin. A separate peace treaty would then be entered into between the Soviet Union and its German satellite. In most of the Western news media concerning the German problem since the crisis of August 1961, the implication of the Soviet Union's proposal over Berlin has been made sufficiently clear—though not always. Yet, therein lies the chief danger to Western strategy on Germany as a whole.

The Berlin problem is a consequence of the division of Germany and a just settlement of the Berlin question would be achieved automatically by reunification. This has induced the Soviets to try to formalize the partition of Germany by changing the present status of West Berlin and making it into a "free city." Once agreement was reached that West Berlin would become a separate political entity, it would imply the surrender of Western aims to reunite Germany, and Communist objectives would be further advanced.

The armed forces of the Western Allies in West Berlin do not constitute a military threat to the Soviet Zone or the Soviet Union. There are about 11,000 military personnel stationed there, and they are surrounded by twenty-two Soviet divisions and the armed forces of the Soviet Zone itself. During their more than twenty years in West Berlin, the Western troops have never committed an act of provocation, nor have they been accused of any by the Soviet government.

Being under the protection of the Western powers, West Berlin has no troops of its own and there are no troops of the Federal Republic stationed there. This is in sharp contrast with the massive military forces of the Soviet which are stationed in East Berlin under the guise of its being the capital of the Soviet Zone. These forces, with tank units, often parade through East Berlin in Communist demonstrations. They were also deployed along the Sector border when the Wall was erected. Soviet authorities cannot pretend that the small number of Western Allied troops presents a military security risk.

In November 1961, when the German Federal Chancellor, Dr. Adenauer, went to Washington for talks with the President of the United States, President Kennedy stated that there are three vital interests in Berlin which the United States will defend:

1. The presence of troops of the three Western powers in Berlin;
2. Free access to Berlin; and
3. The freedom and viability of Berlin.

In his declaration of policy before the lower house of the Parliament on November 29, 1961, Dr. Adenauer stated that negotiations on Berlin offered a prospect of success only if the following principles were observed:

1. The security of the Federal Republic;
2. The maintenance of the existing political, legal and economic ties between Berlin and the Federal Republic, including free access between the two areas for the civilian population; and
3. The upholding of the common Western policy on Germany—reunification, non-recognition of the Soviet Zone regime, and settlement of the frontier questions in a peace treaty with an all-German government.

If the Western will to resist Soviet aggression continues to be convincing, it is unlikely that the Soviet Union would try to take West Berlin by force. It is likely, however, that they will try measures short of war which might involve the possibility of Berlin's withering away. This is what is behind the Soviet proposal for a so-called "free city." It is also why it is essential for the survival of West Berlin as an island of freedom behind the Iron Curtain that its ties with the Federal Republic must be preserved.

The combination of Berlin's vulnerability and the division of Germany is a crucial problem of the world today. Berlin is an outpost of the Free World's defenses against the expansionist program of the Communist bloc. As the traditional capital of a United Germany, the maintenance of a free Berlin is of vital importance in sustaining the national morale of Germany as represented by the Federal Republic.

In turn, the Federal Republic plays a major role in contemporary world politics since West Germany and France are the strongest nations on the European continent after the Soviet Union. Industrially, West Germany is the fourth ranking nation in the world. Although NATO is the defense force which has prevented Communist expansion in Europe, it would inevitably become less effective without Germany because NATO's defense concept would be untenable without the territory of the Federal Republic and its armed forces. At the same time, there is virtually no one who does not believe that if Western Europe needs to be defended by arms, the principal nuclear weapons will be those of the unintegrated United States Strategic Air Command.

If Berlin were to be abandoned by the Western powers and the Soviets were successful in separating the traditional capital from its people, the Soviet Union would achieve a major objective of Communist world strategy. However, surrendering to Soviet demands would be incompatible with agreements that have been confirmed repeatedly by the Western powers since the end of World War II.

In return for Germany's contribution to the defense of the West and its promise never to use armed force to achieve the reunification of Germany, the three Western powers have committed themselves to the cause of German reunification. In particular, they agreed not to recognize the division of Germany but to deal with the Federal Republic as the only legitimate German government. These mutual commitments between the Western powers and the Federal Republic are the basic foundation for German adherence to the Atlantic Community. Without them the German government would have been unable to rally parliamentary support for its membership in NATO. It would be inconceivable for any nation to enter into a partnership in which its partners would negotiate the division of its historic entity on behalf of an avowedly hostile third party.

The basic alliance between the West and Germany, represented by the Federal Republic, is contained in the Paris Treaties of October 1954. The ratification of the Paris Treaties was the culmination of a comprehensive and passionate debate in West Germany because a particularly grave decision was involved. In a note of March 10, 1952, the Soviets held out the possibility of reunification to the German people in return for a commitment on the part of Germany to neutrality and isolation. Had the German people accepted the Soviet bait, NATO would be without German support today. To be sure, the Federal Republic was acting in its own national interests. Uncompromisingly hostile to Communism, it was protecting its own existence by becoming part of the general strengthening of the Free World as a barrier to Soviet encroachment. Nevertheless, entering into a partnership with the Western powers and participating in common programs with other Western European nations has possibly been at the price of achieving national unity.

The Federal Republic has faithfully carried out its obligations under its decision. Even the die-hard opponents of the Republic agree that the German commitment to the West has been one of whole-hearted dedication. There has been no development of the chauvinism that so many of the Federal Republic cirtics feared. Neo-Nazi movements have been limited to the extreme fringe of national life. No country has a better record than Germany in honoring all the duties that fall upon a NATO member. Germany made a great choice, tied her destiny to an equal association with the Atlantic Community, and put aside the policies that could so easily have been dictated by an inflamed nationalism seeking a war of revenge.

Three U.S. Secretaries of State (Dean Acheson, John Foster Dulles and Christian A. Herter) placed the necessity of incorporating a resurgent West Germany in the system of Atlantic defense as a top priority of U.S. policy. They were sometimes accused of placing too much reliance on Germany, of deferring to the wishes of the Bonn government on the most important issues of the Alliance, and of giving West Germany too much power and influence when she still had to justify herself as a genuine democracy. Time and experience have shown these fears and suspicions to be groundless. West Germany's record in NATO is the best answer to these criticisms.

The communiqués issued by the Western Heads of State and Government in December 1959 and the NATO Ministerial Council in May 1962 renewed NATO pledges to Berlin and Germany. They reaffirmed the principles set forth in the Communiqué by the Foreign Ministers of France, the Federal Republic of Germany, the United Kingdom, and the United States of December 14, 1958, and in the Declaration of the North Atlantic Council of December 16, 1958, on Berlin. Paragraph 5 of the latter states:

The Council recalls the responsibility which each member-state has assumed in regard to the security and welfare of Berlin and the maintenance of the position of the three Powers in that city. The member-states of NATO could not approve a solution of the Berlin question which jeopardized the right of the three Western Powers to remain in Berlin as long as their responsibilities require it and did not assure freedom of communication between that city and the Free World. The Soviet Union would be responsible for any action which had the effect of hampering this free communication or endangering this freedom.

For the people of East Berlin and East Germany, the special status of Berlin holds the hope of their eventual reunion with the people of the Federal Republic in a united, democratic German nation. For many of them, until August 13, 1961, West Berlin was an opening in the prison wall which could be visited from time to time for a brief glance into the Free World. For those of them who could no longer endure the tyranny of Communism, it was an escape route to freedom. For all the people held in captivity in the vast detention camp of Eastern Europe, West Berlin is a beacon of hope, nourished since 1948 by the ability of the Western Allies—and West Berliners themselves—to maintain the city's freedom.

For the Western Allies, West Berlin is the symbol, the evidence, and the acid test of their unity, strength and determination. It has become practically a keystone in the defensive arch of NATO. If the Western Allies were to permit the freedom of West Berlin to be lost by direct assault or by erosion, who would respect their pledges in the future? And if they who are the backbone of the security of the Free World should falter and fall apart, what hope for freedom would remain?

Thus, it is apparent that Berlin is a focal point in the East-West world-wide struggle. In the words of the U.S. Secretary of State, Dean Rusk, the central issue in that struggle is ". . . the announced determination to impose a world of coercion upon those not already subjected to it. . . . At stake is the survival and growth of the world of free choice and . . . free cooperation." That central issue, he pointed out, "is posed between the Sino-Soviet empire and all the rest, whether allied or neutral; and it is now posed in every continent."

Late in March 1966, a change in West Germany's foreign policy became apparent when Chancellor Ludwig Erhard dramatically made public a diplomatic note which he had sent to governments around the world. While it was obviously intended in part to refute some of the anti-German sentiment sure to be expressed by leaders of the Communist Party during its 23d Congress in Moscow in April 1966, it nevertheless contained ideas which heretofore had been regarded in Bonn as amounting to heresy. Whatever practical effect it may have in the near future remains to be seen; nevertheless, West Germany's appeal for new and far-reaching security agreements in Central Europe reflects a significant foreign policy change. The former rigidity of the Adenauer era appears to have given way to a more flexible approach to the problem of German reunification.

The gist of the policy is that a final settlement of Europe's problem, including the Berlin question and German reunification, depends on an improvement in Germany's relations with the nations of Eastern Europe, the removal of any fears of a revived aggressive German militarism, and a gradual raising of the Iron Curtain.

The West German proposals are tailored to these goals. The offer to sign a series of bilateral non-aggression pacts with the Soviet Union and the nations of Eastern Europe is a reassuring response to Communist charges of "German revanchism." The Bonn note appears to be addressed more to the small Soviet bloc nations rather than to the Soviet Union itself. It particularly expressed a desire for better relations with Poland and Czechoslovakia, who are the least cordial of West Germany's close neighbors.

The Bonn note hints that West Germany might be ready to guarantee Poland's permanent possession of the former German territories east of the Oder-Neisse Rivers in return for the reunification of Germany. Bonn still claims that Germany's eastern border is a question to be negotiated only with the government of a united Germany. At the same time, the note makes clear that German territorial claims beyond the present Oder-Neisse border would not stand in the way of an agreement based on reason. Bonn admits that, as far as Czechoslovakia is concerned, the 1938 Munich agreement ceding the Sudeten region to Germany was "torn asunder by Hitler" and no longer has "any territorial significance." The West German government does not accept the Czechoslovak contention that the original agreement itself was illegal.

The note also proposed that all non-nuclear nations, Eastern and Western, follow West Germany's example and renounce both the manufacture and acquisition of nuclear weapons and accept international control of non-military nuclear development. Existing nuclear powers are urged to pledge themselves not to turn over weapons to the control of any other country. This pledge would not eliminate plans for nuclear sharing within NATO, in which Bonn has an active interest. Thus, on the control of nuclear weapons, West Germany has adopted the position of the Western nations at the Geneva Disarmament Conference.

Any immediate lessening of Communist hostility or reduction of tension is certainly not to be expected. However, West Germany appears to be moving toward establishing a lasting detente in Europe, and is seeking ways and means which offer the greatest hope for a lasting settlement.

Late in April 1966, East German Communist chief Ulbricht announced his ideas on any reunification plan for East and West Germany. Speaking to an assembly of his Socialist Unity Party, he stated: "Without doubt much in West Germany would have to be changed before the process of union between the two German states and the special territory of West Berlin could be begun." Among these changes, Ulbricht said that prior steps must include disarmament and the renunciation of nuclear arms by East and West Germany, and the recognition by West Germany of the Oder-Neisse frontier with Poland. He also included nationalization of large estates and industries, but stated that those persons who had served peace and understanding since 1945 could keep up to 375 acres of land. Losses by company stockholders could be repaid out of armament funds.

Ulbricht also said that whoever supports the idea of a unified Germany within the "alliance system of the U.S. imperialists in NATO, or even as a part of a Bonn-Washington axis, has in truth written off German reunification." He described a "confederation" as the only remaining way to overcome the division of Germany and added that East Germany was preparing itself for the time when the confederation was a reality.

In Bonn, Chancellor Erhard and representatives of the political parties making up the government coalition agreed to meet with opposition Socialists, led by West Berlin Mayor Willy Brandt, and other representatives of the Socialist Party to work together on a new, non-partisan approach to German unification.

Meanwhile, a serious situation within NATO has arisen in regard to French participation and intentions. What effect this will have on the future of Germany, and on the Western World, cannot now be determined.

The outcome of these developments, however, is being closely followed by the governments of the Western nations and Communist bloc countries alike.

Chapter XI

Summing Up

Since the end of World War II, the governmental status of Berlin has been unique in history. It has been the headquarters for four occupation regimes—the Allied Control Authority for Germany, the Allied Kommandatura, the Soviet Control Commission for Berlin, and the Unilateral Soviet Control Commission for Germany—and four major governmental units—the initial post-hostilities administration of Berlin, the East German Democratic Republic government, the Government of East Berlin, and the Government of West Berlin. There have been in addition four unilateral Allied occupation administrations and twenty city boroughs. Each element of government has had its own authority and administrative structure.

During the post-war years, the inhabitants of Berlin have been subjected to the normal stresses and strains of living in a large metropolitan community, but these pale into insignificance in comparison to the additional physical, psychological and ideological pressures they have endured. They have had to cope with the terrific destruction of Berlin during the war, and resultant task of reconstruction, the psychology of defeat, changing forms of government, and the disposition of thousands of displaced Germans. Further, Berliners were under periods of great tension caused by their geographical isolation from the West, the uncertain means of travel through miles of communist-controlled territory, and from various economic, political and financial crises.

Thus, Berlin has come to be regarded by the Soviets as a primary instrument in its diplomatic maneuvering with the Western powers. The division of Berlin resulted in the creation of two separrate and hostile constitutions, governments, political parties and ideological orientations. Furthermore, the Berlin issue is not a municipal government problem or solely a Federal Republic one. Instead, it has become one of the most crucial problems in East-West relations since World War II. While the Western powers and the Soviet Union agree that the present situation is extremely unusual, neither wishes to resolve it except on its own terms and to its own advantage.

The Western nations would solve the Berlin problem by unifying Germany through free elections, which would have the effect of establishing a free, democratic Germany under a noncommunist government and aligned with the West. On the other side, the Soviets intend to solve the problem by establishing a reunified but communist country, having a reunited Berlin as its capital. Failing this, the Soviets would probably settle for a permanently divided Germany if it were able to force the Western Allies to move out of West Berlin. Then, reunited Berlin would become the capital of East Germany. If these measures fail, the Soviet Union would likely accept a divided Germany and a divided Berlin if it were able to gain control of West Berlin through its "free city" proposition. Undoubtedly, there are other possibilities for resolving the problem, but any departure from the legal position is precarious, and any attempt to use military force to effect a change is extremely hazardous to the peace of the world.

West Berlin is a symbol of hope for the captive people detained within all communist-dominated countries. This is the reason why Khrushchev referred to West Berlin as a "cancerous tumor" and a "bone stuck in our throat," and publicly announced his resolve "to eradicate this splinter from the heart of Europe." There is no reason to believe that Khrushchev's successors in the Kremlin feel any differently. The Western powers regard West Berlin as a showcase of individual enterprise and a testing place of courage and determination while the Soviet Union considers it an instrument for international blackmail. But no matter how it is viewed, the Berlin issue is a part of the communist challenge to the Free World in the struggle for a reunited Germany and, consequently, for the control of Europe. At the same time, West Berlin has become a proving ground of international law as an instrument of civilized governments.

Since the end of World War II, the Soviet Union has initiated a number of Berlin crises in an effort to force the Western Allies out of Berlin. Such action, if successful, would in effect acknowledge the

West's inability to cope with the Soviet Union's military might and its communist ideology. The first major test occurred during 1948 when the communists initiated the Berlin blockade. The reaction of the Western powers forced the communists to back down. In November, ten years later, Khrushchev created the second Berlin crisis by issuing an ultimatum demanding the withdrawal of occupation forces, the establishment of West Berlin as a demilitarized "free city" and the proposal that "the two German states" enter into negotiations looking toward a confederation—without free elections in the East Zone. The Soviet note set a deadline of six months and stated that if the Western Allies had not acceded to its demands by then, the Soviet Union would sign a separate peace treaty with the German Democratic Republic and turn over to it control of all access routes to Berlin. The Western Allies firmly rejected the Soviet note and again the Russians backed down.

Following the shooting down of the U.S. reconnaissance plane over Soviet territory in May, 1960, and the failure of the Paris Summit Conference, the communists began a series of harassing actions which included stopping West German visitors to Berlin at the Zonal frontier and protesting civilian air transportation from the West into Berlin. As counter measures, the Western Allies and the Federal Republic prohibited communist functionaries from entering West Berlin and West Germany, and canceled the inter-Zonal trade agreement on September 30, 1960. Again the communists backed down.

In 1961, the Soviet Union resumed its diplomatic offensive against the status of Berlin. The Soviet aide memoire of June 4, 1961, which was handed to President Kennedy by Khrushchev during their meeting in Vienna, emphasized the determination of the Soviet Union to resolve the questions of Berlin and Germany in her own way, with complete disregard of prior binding agreements and international law. Khrushchev tried to force the conclusion of a peace treaty before the end of 1961 by threatening with the nuclear strength of the Soviet Union. Moscow's ultimatum was followed by more threats—to cut off lines of communication with the West, political and economic pressures in the Soviet Zone, and communist measures against the more than 50,000 East Berliners who held jobs in West Berlin.

On July 25, 1961, President Kennedy delivered a Report to the

Nation on the Berlin crisis from the White House by television and radio. Referring to West Berlin, he stated: ". . . But above all it has now become, as never before, the great testing place of Western courage and will, a focal point where our solemn commitments, stretching back over the years since 1945, and Soviet ambitions now meet in basic confrontation. . . . We must meet our oft-stated pledge to the free peoples of West Berlin—and maintain our rights and their safety, even in the face of force—in order to maintain the confidence of other free peoples in our word and our resolve."

But the sector boundary between East and West Berlin was closed at about 2:00 a.m. on August 13, 1961, and the building of the Infamous Wall of Berlin was begun.

Each of the three major Berlin crises was but one move by the Communists in furtherance of the attainment of their goal of world domination in the Cold War battle. Essentially, the demands made in the Soviet note of November 1958 and the Aide Memoire of June 1965 were the same, namely: the withdrawal of Western military forces from West Berlin, creation of West Berlin as a demilitarized "free city," and conclusion of a German peace settlement. In addition, however, the Soviet Union entertains additional and very tangible objectives: frustrate the Western powers by continued harassment and crises, create suspicion and unrest among Western nations, separate West Germany from the Western Allies, and break up NATO.

The objectives of the Western Allies have been repeatedly affirmed: uphold their legal rights in Berlin, maintain armed forces in West Berlin as long as required, consider an armed attack on West Berlin as an attack upon themselves, protect the freedom and viability of West Berlin, and seek reunification of the city—and Germany —through free elections.

In the fall of 1962, the Berlin crisis was overshadowed by other tensions in international politics when the United States discovered that the Soviet Union was in the process of developing Cuba as a military base for nuclear missiles. The United States emerged from this test of will and determination strengthened with a considerable gain in international prestige. The U.S. fully demonstrated its resolution not to be blackmailed by threats of war, which were one of the most important weapons of the Soviet Union during the Berlin crises.

Late in April, 1966, the Federal Republic issued a 562-page White

Paper containing 193 documents which described its futile efforts to achieve the reunification of Germany during the past decade. The book followed Bonn's peace note which was described in the previous chapter and it was also aimed at what Chancellor Erhard described as "slanderous propaganda" against West Germany.

The White Paper is a partial record of the diplomatic efforts of the Western Allies and the Federal Republic to further unification since the Geneva Conference of 1955. It is interesting that it includes no mention of the numerous conversations between former Chancellor Adenauer and the long-time Soviet ambassador to Bonn, Andrei Smirnov, nor those held by Khrushchev with Adenauer's one-time envoy, Hans Kroll.

The book illustrates the remarkable continuity of the Bonn government policy-makers in upholding the same line for more than a decade, despite numerous pressures, changes and opportunities arising in both the East and the West. It also shows how Bonn's interest in arms control, relaxation of tensions, and a dialogue with the East have varied directly with the pressure applied from the West. The Geneva Conference of 1955, the Camp David meeting of Khrushchev and President Eisenhower, and President Kennedy's search for a dialogue in 1961 and 1963 each compelled Bonn to join in the peace effort. However, once the pressure was off, Bonn came up with no new ideas of its own until its peace note of March 1966.

The prospects for East-West political debates between West German Social Democrats and East German Communists, described in the previous chapter, were put in doubt late in April 1966. A few hours after negotiators from the Social Democratic Party crossed into East Berlin for first-round discussions designed to make the necessary arrangements for the unprecedented debates, the official East German news agency reported that communist leader Ulbricht wanted a postponement of the debates to an indefinite date in the future.

The realities of the German problem are even more complex than they are generally understood to be, and no single aspect should be considered separately from the others. Behind the power rivalry between the East and West lie the totalitarian practice of communist ideology on one hand and the example of freedom and justice on the other. Behind these opposing philosophies and their execution, lies the commitment of each side to defend its ideal realities, morally and physically—a defense in which the Federal Republic is called upon to make its limited but not unimportant contribution to the West.

It can be stated with considerable truth that if the communists did not push their ideological world-domination program, there would be no Berlin Wall and no Berlin crises—because there is no serious problem in the status of the city that could not be resolved amicably by reasonable people. The resolution of the problem depends entirely on the desire of the people and nations involved to attain such a goal. In this vital East-West struggle, the amazing and heartening thing is the ability of the West Berliners to maintain their equilibrium and to prosper during a crisis-filled era. But, long accustomed to living with uncertainty and paradox, West Berliners courageously face the continuation of the temporary-permanent situation which has been the fate of their city since the end of World War II and for which, at the moment, there is no end in sight.

The Infamous Wall still stands, a hideous monument to communist failure, for it was built not to protect the East German peoples from their enemies but to keep them forcibly confined in a state of totalitarian captivity.

Appendix I

Protocol between the Governments of the United States of America, the United Kingdom, and the Union of Soviet Socialist Republics on the zones of occupation in Germany and the administration of Greater Berlin of September 9, 1944.

The Governments of the United States of America, the United Kingdom of Great Britain and Northern Ireland, and the Union of Soviet Socialist Republics have reached the following agreement with regard to the execution of Article 11 of the Instrument of Unconditional Surrender of Germany:—

1. Germany, within her frontiers as they were on the 31st December, 1937, will, for the purposes of occupation, be divided into three zones, one of which will be allotted to each of the three Powers, *and a special Berlin area,* which will be under joint occupation by the three Powers.

2. The boundaries of the three zones and of the Berlin area, and the allocation of the three zones as between the U.S.A., the U.K. and the U.S.S.R. will be as follows:—

Eastern Zone

The territory of Germany (including the province of East Prussia) situated to the East of a line drawn from the point on Lubeck Bay where the frontiers of Schleswig-Holstein and Mecklenburg meet, along the western frontier of Mecklenburg to the frontier of the province Hanover, thence, along the eastern frontier of Hanover to the frontier of Brunswick; thence along the western frontier of the Prussian province of Saxony to the western frontier of Anhalt; thence along the western frontier of Anhalt; thence along the western frontier of the Prussian province of Saxony and the western frontier of Thuringia to where the latter meets the Bavarian frontier;

thence eastwards along the northern frontier of Bavaria to the 1937 Czechoslovakian frontier, will be occupied by armed forces of the U.S.S.R., *with the exception of the Berlin area, for which a special system of occupation is provided below.*

North-Western Zone

The territory of Germany situated to the west of the line defined above, and bounded on the south by a line drawn from the point where the western frontier of Thuringia meets the frontier of Bavaria; thence westwards along the southern frontiers of the Prussian provinces of Hessen-Nassau and Rheinprovinz to where the latter meets the frontier of France will be occupied by armed forces of . . .

South-Western Zone

All the remaining territory of Western Germany situated to the south of the line defined in the description of the North-Western Zone will be occupied by armed forces of . . .

The frontiers of States (Laender) and Provinces within Germany, referred to in the foregoing descriptions of the zones, are those which existed after the coming into effect of the decree of June 25th, 1941 (published in the Reichsgesetzblatt, Part I No. 72, July 3rd, 1941.)

Berlin Area

The Berlin area (by which expression is understood the territory of "Greater Berlin" as defined by the Law of April 27th, 1920) will be jointly occupied by armed forces of the U.S.A., U.K., and U.S.S.R., assigned by the respective Commanders-in-Chief. For this purpose the territory of "Greater Berlin" will be divided into the following three parts:—

North-Eastern part of "Greater Berlin" (districts of Pankow, Prenzlauerberg, Mitte, Weissensee, Friedrichshain, Lichtenberg, Treptow, Kopenick) will be occupied by the forces of the U.S.S.R.:

North-Western part of "Greater Berlin" (districts of Reinickendorf, Wedding, Tiergarten, Charlottenburg, Spandau, Wilmersdorf) will be occupied by the forces of . . .

Southern part of "Greater Berlin" (districts of Zehlendorf, Steglitz, Schöneberg, Kreuzberg, Tempelhof, Neukölln) will be occupied by the forces of . . .

The boundaries of districts within "Greater Berlin," referred to in the foregoing descriptions, are those which existed after the coming into effect of the decree published on March 27th, 1938 (Amsblatt der Reichshauptstadt Berlin No. 13 of March 27th, 1938, page 215).

3. The occupying forces in each of the three zones into which Germany is divided will be under a Commander-in-Chief designated by the Government of the country whose forces occupy that zone.

4. Each of the three Powers may, at its discretion, include among the forces assigned to occupation duties under the command of its Commander-in-Chief, auxiliary contingents from the forces of any other Allied Power which has participated in military operations against Germany.

5. An Inter-Allied Governing Authority (Kommandatura) consisting of three Commandants, appointed by their respective Commanders-in-Chief, will be established to direct jointly the administration of the "Greater Berlin" Area.

6. This Protocol has been drawn up in triplicate in the English and Russian languages. Both texts are authentic. The Protocol will come into force on the signature by Germany of the Instrument of Unconditional Surrender.

The above text of the Protocol between the Governments of the United States of America, the United Kingdom and the Union of Soviet Socialist Republics, on the zones of occupation in Germany and the administration of "Greater Berlin" has been prepared and unanimously adopted by the European Advisory Commission at a meeting held on September 12th, 1944, with the exception of the allocation of the North-Western and South-Western zones of occupation in Germany and the North-Western and Southern parts of "Greater Berlin" which requires further consideration and joint agreement by the Governments of the U.S.A., U.K. and U.S.S.R.

Appendix II

Agreement on Control Machinery in Germany—Excerpts—Nov. 14, 1944

The Governments of the United States of America, the United Kingdom of Great Britain and Northern Ireland and the Union of Soviet Socialist Republics have reached the following Agreement with regard to the organization of the Allied control machinery in Germany in the period during which Germany will be carrying out the basic requirements of unconditional surrender:—

Article 1. Supreme authority in Germany will be exercised, on instructions from their respective Governments, by the Commanders-in-Chief of the armed forces of the United States of America, the United Kingdom and the Union of Soviet Socialist Republics, each in his own zone of occupation, and also jointly, in matters affecting Germany as a whole, in their capacity as members of the supreme organ of control constituted under the present Agreement.

. . .

Article 3. (a) The three Commanders-in-Chief, acting together as a body, will constitute a supreme organ of control called the Control Council.

(b) The functions of the Control Council will be:

. . .

(ii) to initiate plans and reach agreed decisions on the chief military, political, economic and other questions affecting Germany as a whole, on the basis of instructions received by each Commander-in-Chief from his Government;

(iii) to control the German central administration, which will operate under the direction of the Control Council and will be responsible to it for ensuring compliance with its demands;

(iv) to direct the administration of "Greater Berlin" through appropriate organs.

Article 4. A permanent Co-ordinating Committee will be established under the Control Council, composed of one representative of each of the three Commanders-in-Chief, not below the rank of General Officer or the equivalent rank in the naval or air forces. Members of the Co-ordinating Committee will, when necessary, attend meetings of the Control Council.

. . .

Article 6. (a) The members of the Control Staff, appointed by their respective national authorities, will be organized in the following Divisions:—

Military; Naval; Air; Transport; Political; Economic; Finance; Reparation, Deliveries and Restitution; Internal Affairs and Communications; Legal; Prisoners of War and Displaced Persons; Man-power.

Adjustments in the number and functions of the Divisions may be made in the light of experience.

. . .

Article 7. (a) An inter-Allied Governing Authority (Komendatura) consisting of three commandants, one from each Power, appointed by their respective Commanders-in-Chief, will be established to direct jointly the administration of the "Greater Berlin" area. Each of the Commandants will serve in rotation, in the position of Chief Commandant, as head of the Inter-Allied Governing Authority.

. . .

Article 10. The Allied organs for the control and administration of Germany outlined above will operate during the initial period of the occupation of Germany immediately following surrender, that is, the period when Germany is carrying out the basic requirements of unconditional surrender.

Article 11. The question of the Allied organs required for carrying out the functions of control and administration in Germany in a later period will be the subject of a separate Agreement between the Governments of the United States of America, the United Kingdom and the Union of Soviet Socialist Republics.

The above text of the Agreement on Control Machinery in Germany between the Governments of the United States of America, the United Kingdom and the Union of Soviet Socialist Republics has been prepared and unanimously adopted by the Representatives of the United States of America, the United Kingdom and the Union of Soviet Socialist Republics on the European Advisory Commission at a meeting held on 14th November, 1944, and is now submitted to their respective Governments for approval.

Appendix III

Temporary Constitution of Greater Berlin, Approved by the Allied Kommandatura Berlin on August 13, 1946—Excerpts

The Allied Commandants consider that the restoration of constitutional government to the city of Berlin is a historic occasion. In forwarding this document to the Magistrat with the order of the Allied Kommandatura the occupation forces reiterate their purpose to establish political independence in Berlin and to restore to the people the right of self-determination in their government. . . . This constitution of 1946 is a temporaray document intended to restore political freedom and place it in the hands of the people of Berlin. . . . The Allied Commandants have authorized this new Constitution to become effective in October at which time elections will be held and they place the responsibility for the government of Berlin, under the Allied Kommandatura, in the hands of the people of the city confident that democratic processes will never again be abandoned.

Appendix IV

Report on the Berlin (Potsdam) Conference of the Three Heads of Government, August 2, 1945—Excerpts

III. Germany

. . .

It is not the intention of the Allies to destroy or enslave the German people. It is the intention of the Allies that the German people be given the opportunity to prepare for the eventual reconstruction of their life on a democratic and peaceful basis. If their own efforts are steadily directed to this end, it will be possible for them in due course to take their place among the free and peaceful peoples of the world.

The Political and Economic Principles to Govern the Treatment of Germany in the Initial Control Period

A. Political Principles

. . .

9. I. Local self-government shall be restored throughout Germany on democratic principles and in particular through elective councils as rapidly as is consistent with military security and the purposes of military occupation.

9. II. All democratic political parties with rights of assembly and of public discussion shall be allowed and encouraged throughout Germany;

. . .

B. Economic Principles

. . .

14. During the period of occupation Germany shall be treated as a single economic unit.

. . .

19. Payment of Reparations should leave enough resources to enable the German people to subsist without external assistance. In working out the economic balance of Germany the necessary means must be provided to pay for imports approved by the Control Council in Germany. The proceeds of exports from current production and stock shall be available in the first place for payment for such imports.

. . .

VI. City of Koenigsberg and the Adjacent Area

The Conference examined a proposal by the Soviet Government that pending the final determination of territorial questions at the peace settlement, the section of the western frontier of the Union of Soviet Socialist Republics which is adjacent to the Baltic Sea should pass from a point on the eastern shore of the Bay of Danzig to the east, north of Braunsberg-Goldap, to the meeting point of the frontiers of Lithuania, the Polish Republic and East Prussia.

. . .

IX. Poland

. . .

The three Heads of Government reaffirm their opinion that the final delimitation of the western frontier of Poland should await the peace settlement.

. . .

Appendix V

Quadripartite Statement on Control Machinery in Germany, June 5, 1945—Excerpts

1. In the period when Germany is carrying out the basic requirements of unconditional surrender, supreme authority in Germany will be exercised, on instructions from their Governments, by the Soviet, British, United States, and French Commanders-in-Chief, each in his own zone of occupation, and also jointly, in matters affecting Germany as a whole. The four Commanders-in-Chief will together constitute the Control Council. Each Commander-in-Chief will be assisted by a political adviser.

2. The Control Council, whose decisions shall be unanimous, will ensure appropriate uniformity of action by the Commanders-in-Chief in their respective zones of occupation and will reach agreed decisions on the chief questions affecting Germany as a whole.

3. Under the Control Council, there will be a permanent Coordinating Committee composed of one representative of each of the four Commanders-in-Chief and Control Staff organized in the following Divisions (which are subject to adjustment in the light of experience):

> Military; Naval; Air; Transport; Political; Economic; Finance; Reparation, Deliveries and Restitution; Internal Affairs and Communications; Legal; Prisoners of War and Displaced Persons; Manpower.

There will be four heads of each Division, one designated by each Power. The staffs of the Divisions may include civilian as well as military personnel, and may also in special cases include nationals of other United Nations appointed in a personal capacity.

. . .

7. The administration of the "Greater Berlin" area will be directed by an Inter-Allied Governing Authority, which will operate under the general direction of the Control Council, and will consist of four Commandants, each of whom will serve in rotation as Chief Commandant. They will be assisted by a technical staff which will supervise and control the activities of the local German organs.

8. The arrangements outlined above will operate during the period of occupation following German surrender, when Germany is carrying out the basic requirements of unconditional surrender. Arrangements for the subsequent period will be the subject of a separate agreement.

Appendix VI

Allied Agreement on Quadripartite Administration of Berlin, July 7, 1945

In accordance with Article 7 of the Agreement on the Allied Control Machinery in Germany, the Conference of the Representatives of the Allied Commands held in Berlin on the 7 July 1945 passed the following resolution:

1. For the purpose of exercising the joint administration of Berlin, an Inter-Allied Military Commandatura is to be established under a Chief Military Commandant, whose duties are to be performed by each of the Military Commandants of the Allied Military Commandaturas of Berlin in turn during a period of 15 days.

The Chief Military Commandant will exercise the administration of all Berlin zones, utilizing for this purpose conferences of the Allied Military Commandants to solve questions of principle and problems common to all zones. The resolutions of such conferences are to be passed unanimously.

Orders and instructions of the Chief Military Commandant of Berlin issued in the Russian, English, French, and German languages will be transmitted to the Oberbuergermeister of Berlin and must be obeyed in all zones of the City.

2. For the purpose of ensuring the supervision of Berlin and the coordination of the administration among the zones, a Headquarters of the Chief Military Commandant of Berlin consisting of Allied Representatives is to be established. In order to exercise the supervision and control of Berlin local government, one or two representatives from each Allied Commandatura are to be attached to every section of local government.

3. The Allied Military Commandatura of Berlin will organize the administration in their respective zones in conformity with the orders

of the Chief Military Commandant, taking into account local conditions.

4. The first conference of the Inter-Allied Military Commandatura is to be held on 11 July, with the Soviet Military Commandant in the chair.

5. The present resolution is done in the Russian and English languages and shall come into force on signing.

Appendix VII

Declaration by Western Commandants to Continue Operation of Kommandatura December 21, 1948

On July 1st, the Soviet Authorities withdrew from the Allied Kommandatura and thus disrupted the quadripartite administration of Berlin.

The Allied Kommandatura was established by agreements concluded between the four Governments, which can only be altered or abrogated by agreement of all the Governments which were party to them. The Allied Kommandatura has not, therefore, ceased to exist, although its work has, since July 1st, been in suspense owing to the refusal of the Soviet Authorities to attend its meetings.

The Temporary Constitution of Berlin, which was approved by all four Allies in 1946, requires that legislation and certain other acts of the Magistrat and City Assembly shall receive Allied approval. The refusal of the Soviet Authorities to attend meetings of the Allied Kommandatura cannot any longer be allowed to obstruct the proper administration of Berlin, according to the law.

The Allied Kommandatura will therefore resume its work forthwith. If the Soviet Authorities, either now or at a future date, decide to abide by the agreements to which the four Powers are committed, the quadripartite administration of Berlin could be resumed. During their abstentions the three Western Allies will exercise the powers of the Allied Kommandatura although it is realized that owing to Soviet obstruction it will only be possible for them to carry out their decisions in the Western Sectors for the present.

Appendix VIII

Statement of Principles Governing the Relationship between the Allied Kommandatura and Greater Berlin, 14 May 1949

1. (a) Greater Berlin shall have, subject only to the limitations set out in this statement, full legislative and executive and judicial powers in accordance with the Temporary Constitution of 1946 or with any subsequent Constitution adopted by the City Assembly and approved by the Allied Kommandatura in accordance with the provisions of this statement;

(b) Article 36 of the Temporary Constitution of Berlin will be held in suspense and BK/$0_{(47)34}$ and BK/$0_{(47)56}$ which were issued in implementation of that article, will be annulled.

2. In order to ensure the accomplishment of the basic purpose of Occupation, powers in the following fields are specifically reserved to the Allied Kommandatura, including the right to request and verify information and statistics needed by the Occupation Authorities.

(a) Disarmament and demilitarization, including related fields of scientific research, prohibitions and restrictions on industry and civil aviation;

(b) Restitution, reparations, decartelization, deconcentration, non-discrimination in trade matters, foreign interests in Berlin and claims against Berlin, or its inhabitants;

(c) Relations with authorities abroad;

(d) Displaced persons and the admission of refugees;

(e) Protection, prestige and security of Allied Forces, dependents, employees and representatives, their immunities and satisfaction of occupation costs and their other requirements;

(f) Respect for the Temporary Constitution of Berlin of 1946 or of any Constitution which may be approved by the Allied Kommandatura to replace the Temporary Constitution;

(g) Control over foreign trade and exchange;

(h) Control over internal action, only to the minimum extent necessary to ensure use of funds, food and other supplies in such manner as to reduce to a minimum the need for external assistance to Berlin;

(i) Control of the care and treatment in German prisons of persons charged before or sentenced by the courts or tribunals of the Occupying Powers or Occupation Authorities; over the carrying out of sentences imposed on them and other questions of amnesty, pardon or release in relation to them;

(j) Supervision of the Berlin Police, in view of the special circumstances prevailing in Berlin, in a manner to be defined in an additional document, which will be issued by the Allied Kommandatura on this subject . . . ;

(k) Legislation or action tending to restrict the freedom of speech, the press, assembly or association, until such time as these four basic rights are guaranteed by the Berlin Constitution;

(l) Such controls as have been or may be imposed by the Allied Kommandatura to ensure that counter-blockade measures, including measures in connection with the airlift and the restriction of exports, shall remain effective during the continuance of the blockade;

(m) Control of banking, currency and credit policy so that it may be fully coordinated with the banking and credit policies of larger areas of Germany under Allied supervision.

3. (a) It is the hope and expectation of the Commandants that the Occupation Authorities will not have occasion to take action in fields other than those specifically reserved above. The Occupation Authorities, however, reserve the right to resume in whole or in part the exercise of full authority if they consider that to do so is essential to security or to preserve the democratic government, or in pursuance of the international obligations of their Governments. Before doing so, they will formally advise the appropriate Berlin Authorities of their decision and of the reasons therefor;

(b) In addition, in the special circumstances prevailing in Berlin, the Occupation Authorities reserve the right to intervene, in an emergency, and issue orders to ensure the security, good order and financial and economic stability of the City.

4. Greater Berlin shall have the power, after due notification to the Allied Kommandatura, to legislate and act in the fields reserved to

the Allied Kommandatura, except as the Allied Kommandatura itself otherwise specifically directs, or as such legislation or action would be inconsistent with decisions or actions taken by the Occupation Authorities themselves.

5. Any amendment to the Temporary Constitution, any new Constitution approved by the City Assembly designed to replace the Temporary Constitution, any amendment to such new Constitution, or legislation in the fields reserved above will require the express approval of the Allied Kommandatura before becoming effective. All other legislation will become effective 21 days after official receipt by the Allied Kommandatura unless previously disapproved by them provisionally or finally. The Allied Kommandatura will not disapprove such legislation unless, in their opinion, it is inconsistent with the Constitution in force, legislation or other directive of the Occupation Authorities themselves, or the provisions of this statement, or unless it constitutes a grave threat to the basic purposes of the Occupation.

6. Subject only to the requirements of their security, the Occupation Authorities guarantee that all agencies of the Occupation will respect the civil rights of every person to be protected against arbitrary arrest, search, or seizure, to be represented by counsel, to be admitted to appeal as circumstances warrant, to communicate with relatives, and to have a fair prompt trial.

7. Orders and instructions of the Allied Kommandatura or the Sector Military Governments, issued before the date of this statement, shall remain in force until repealed or amended by the Allied Kommandatura or the Sector Military Governments as appropriate in accordance with the following provisions:

(a) The Allied Kommandatura and Sector Military Government orders or instructions relating to reserved subjects will remain in force and will be codified;

(b) The Allied Kommandatura and Sector Military Governments will, as soon as possible, cancel all orders and instructions which are inconsistent with this statement. It may be necessary for certain of these orders and instructions to remain in force until they are replaced by City legislation. In such cases, the Allied Kommandatura or the Sector Military Government, as appropriate, will repeal such orders and instructions on the request of the City Government.

Appendix IX

Instrument of Revision of Statement of Principles, 1951

The Allied Kommandatura hereby promulgates the following modification of the Statement of Principles of May 14, 1949, which, except as modified by this Instrument, continues in force:

I. Paragraph 1 is amended to read as follows:

"1. Berlin shall have, subject only to the limitations set out in this Statement, full legislative and executive and judicial powers in accordance with the Berlin Constitution of 1950 as approved by the Allied Kommandatura on 29 August 1950."

II. The words "non-discrimination in trade matters" are deleted from Paragraph 2(b).

III. Paragraphs 2(c), 2(f), 2(g), and 2(j) are amended to read as follows:

"(c) Relations with authorities abroad, but this power will be exercised so as to permit the Berlin authorities to assure the representation of Berlin interests in this field by suitable arrangements;"

"(f) Respect for the Berlin Constitution of 1950 as approved by the Allied Kommandatura on 29 August 1950;"

"(g) Control over external trade and exchange and over trade between Berlin and the Western Zones of Germany; and control over monetary and fiscal policies insofar only as these policies seriously affect Berlin's need for external assistance;"

"(j) Authority over Berlin police to the extent necessary to ensure the security of Berlin."

IV. Paragraphs 2(h), 2(k), 2(l) and 2(m) are deleted.

V. In Paragraph 4, the word "Berlin" is substituted for "Greater Berlin."

VI. Paragraph 5 is amended to read as follows:

"5. Any amendment of the Berlin Constitution or any new Constitution of Berlin will require the express approval of the Allied Kommandatura before becoming effective. All other legislation will be effective without review by the Allied Kommandatura, but will be subject to repeal or annulment by it. The Allied Kommandatura will not repeal or annul legislation unless, in its opinion, it is inconsistent with the provisions of this Statement of Principles as revised, or with legislation or other measures of the Occupation Authorities, or unless it constitutes a grave threat to the basic purposes of the Occupation."

VII. Paragraph 7 is amended to read as follows:

"7. All Occupation legislation will remain in force until repealed or amended by the Allied Kommandatura or the Sector Commandant concerned. Insofar as legislation of the Allied Kommandatura or the Sector Commandants is not based on the reserved powers, it will be repealed at the request of the appropriate Berlin authorities."

VIII. This Instrument shall become effective on 8th March 1951.

Appendix X

The New York Four Power Agreement on the Lifting of the Berlin Blockade May 4, 1949

The Governments of France, the Union of Soviet Socialist Republics, the United Kingdom, and the United States have reached the following agreement:

1. All the restrictions imposed since March 1, 1948, by the Government of the Union of Soviet Socialist Republics on communications, transportation and trade between Berlin and the Western zones of Germany and between the Eastern zone and the Western zones will be removed on May 12, 1949.

2. All the restrictions imposed since March 1, 1948, by the Governments of France, the United Kingdom, and the United States, or any one of them, on communications, transportation, and trade between Berlin and the Eastern zone and between the Western and Eastern zones of Germany will also be removed on May 12, 1949.

3. Eleven days subsequent to the removal of the restrictions referred to in paragraphs one and two, namely, on May 23, 1949, a meeting of the Council of Foreign Ministers will be convened in Paris to consider questions relating to Germany and problems arising out of the situation in Berlin, including also the question of currency in Berlin.

Appendix XI

Final Communiqué of the Sixth Session of the Council of Foreign Ministers at Paris, June 20, 1949 (Extract)

THE GERMAN QUESTION

Despite the inability at this session of the Council of Foreign Ministers to reach agreement on the restoration of the economic and political unity of Germany the Foreign Ministers of France, the Union of Soviet Socialist Republics, the United Kingdom and the United States will continue their efforts to achieve this result and in particular now agree as follows:

. . .

2. The occupation authorities, in the light of the intention of the Ministers to continue their efforts to achieve the restoration of the economic and political unity of Germany, shall consult together in Berlin on a quadripartite basis.

3. These consultations will have as their purpose, among others, to mitigate the effects of the present administrative division of Germany and of Berlin notably in the matters listed below:

A) Expansion of trade and development of the financial and economic relations between the western zones and the eastern zone and between Berlin and the zones.

B) Facilitation of the movement of persons and goods and the exchange of information between the western zones and the eastern zone and between Berlin and the zones.

C) Consideration of questions of common interest relating to the administration of the four sectors in Berlin with a view to normalizing as far as possible the life of the city.

. . .

5. The Governments of France, the Union of Soviet Socialist Republics, the United Kingdom and the United States agree that the New York Agreement of May 4, 1949 shall be maintained. Moreover, in order to promote further the aims set forth in the preceding paragraphs and in order to improve and supplement this and other arrangements and agreements as regards the movement of persons and goods and communications between the eastern zone and the western zones and between the zones and Berlin and also in regard to transit, the occupation authorities, each in his own zone, will have an obligation to take the measures necessary to ensure the normal functioning and utilization of rail, water, and road transport for such movement of persons and goods and such communications by post, telephone and telegraph.

Appendix XII

Commitments Included in Paris Agreements, October 1954

I. ODER-NEISSE LINE

Commitment of the Federal Republics:

Upon her accession to the North Atlantic Treaty and the Brussels Treaty, the German Federal Republic declares that she will refrain from any action inconsistent with the strictly defensive character of the two treaties. In particular the German Federal Republic undertakes never to have recourse to force to achieve the reunification of Germany or the modification of the present boundaries of the German Federal Republic, and to resolve by peaceful means any disputes which may arise between the Federal Republic and other states. (Annex A, Resolution of Association by other Parties to the North Atlantic Treaty, October 22, 1954.)

Commitment of the Government of the United States, the United Kingdom and France:

A peace settlement for the whole of Germany, freely negotiated between Germany and her former enemies, which should lay the foundation of a lasting peace, remains an essential aim of their policy. The final determination of the boundaries of Germany must await such a settlement. (Annex B, Resolution of Association by other Parties to the North Atlantic Treaty, October 22, 1954.)

Commitment of the other NATO Allies:

The Parties to the North Atlantic Treaty signed at Washington on 4th April, 1949, being satisfied that the security of the North Atlantic area will be enhanced by the accession of the Federal Republic of Germany to that Treaty, and

Having noted that the Federal Republic of Germany has, by a declaration dated 3rd October, 1954, accepted the obligations set forth in Article 2 of the Charter of the United Nations and has undertaken upon its accession to the North Atlantic Treaty to refrain from any action inconsistent with the strictly defensive character of the Treaty, and

Having further noted that all member Governments have associated themselves with the declaration also made on 3rd October, 1954, by the Governments of the United States of America, the United Kingdom of Great Britain and Northern Ireland and the French Republic in connection with the aforesaid declaration of the Federal Republic of Germany,

AGREE as follows:

Upon the entry into force of the present Protocol, the Government of the United States of America shall on behalf of all the Parties communicate to the Government of the Federal Republic of Germany an invitation to accede to the North Atlantic Treaty. Thereafter the Federal Republic of Germany shall become a party to that Treaty on the date when it deposits its instrument of accession with the Government of the United States of America in accordance with Article 10 of the Treaty. (Protocol to the North Atlantic Treaty on the Accession of the Federal Republic of Germany, October 23, 1954.)

II. NON-RECOGNITION OF EAST GERMANY

Commitment of the Federal Republic:

(1) The Federal Republic agrees to conduct its policy in accordance with the principles set forth in the Charter of the United Nations and with the aims defined in the Statute of the Council of Europe.

(2) The Federal Republic affirms its intention to associate itself fully with the community of free nations through membership in international organizations contributing to the common aims of the free world. The Three Powers will support applications for such membership by the Federal Republic at appropriate times. (Article 3, Convention on Relations between the Three Powers and the Federal Republic of Germany, October 23, 1954.)

Commitment of the Governments of the United States, the United Kingdom and France:

The Governments of the United States of America, the United Kingdom of Great Britain and Northern Ireland and the French Republic.

. . .

Take note that the German Federal Republic has by a Declaration dated 3rd October accepted the obligations set forth in Article 2 of the Charter of the United Nations and has undertaken never to have recourse to force to achieve the reunification of Germany or the modification of the present boundaries of the German Federal Republic, and to resolve by peaceful means any disputes which may arise between the Federal Republic and other States;

DECLARE THAT:

1. They consider the Government of the Federal Republic as the only German Government freely and legitimately constituted and therefore entitled to speak for Germany as the representative of the German people in international affairs. (Annex B, Resolution of Association by other Parties to the North Atlantic Treaty, October 22, 1954.)

Commitment of the other NATO Allies:

Same as above.

III. RESTRICTION OF ARMAMENTS

Commitment of the Federal Republic:

The Federal Chancellor declares:

that the Federal Republic undertakes not to manufacture in its territory any atomic weapons, chemical weapons or biological weapons as detailed in paragraphs I, II and III of the attached list:

that it undertakes further not to manufacture in its territory such weapons as those detailed in paragraphs IV, V and VI of the attached list.

Any amendment to or cancellation of the substance of paragraphs IV, V and VI can on the request of the Federal Republic, be carried out by a resolution of the Brussels Council of Ministers by a two-thirds majority if in accordance with the needs of the armed forces a request is made by the competent Supreme Commander of the North Atlantic Treaty Organization;

that the Federal Republic agrees to supervision by the competent authority of the Brussels Treaty Organization to ensure that these undertakings are observed. (Annex I, Protocol No. III on the Control of Armaments, October 23, 1954.)

Commitment of the Governments of the United States, the United Kingdom and France:

In their relations with the Federal Republic they will follow the principles set out in Article 2 of the United Nations Charter. (Annex B, Resolution of Association by other Parties to the North Atlantic Treaty, October 22, 1954.)

The Organization is based on the principle of the sovereign equality of all its Members. (Article 2, Charter of the United Nations.)

Appendix XIII

Note from the Government
of the Union of Soviet Socialist Republics
to the Government of the Federal Republic of Germany
on the Situation of Berlin, November 27, 1958—Excerpts

. . .

The regrettable circumstance that the German question has not yet been settled results directly from the Federal Republic's adherence to NATO policy and its departure, along with the Western Powers, from the principles of the Potsdam Agreement. In fact the German people are today just as far from the re-establishment of their national unity as they were in the first months after the Second World War, and indeed the totally unjustifiable fact that there is still no peace treaty makes this aim even more remote. The Soviet Government sympathizes with those elements among the German people who wish to bring about the reunification of Germany according to peaceful and democratic principles. The Soviet Government can, however, only express its wishes, it cannot exert force on the German people or interfere in German internal affairs. It is also clear, that the Soviet Government cannot acknowledge the right of any other power to impose its will on either of the two German states.

This being the situation, that two German states have arisen with different social systems, the Soviet Government sees no other way to the reunification of Germany than a gradual rapprochement between these two states, which would lead to the establishment of a single state-machinery, i.e. the formation of a German Confederation, as has been suggested by the German Democratic Republic. The longer the Federal Government ignores the Confederation proposal, the more it will be considered as an opponent of German unity. Declarations by German statesmen responsible for the Foreign policy of the Federal Republic that they are anxious to promote this unity do not alter the situation in the least, for they are sufficiently disproved by the facts, by the actual policy of the Federal Government, which only widens the gulf between the two German states.

The Soviet Government has carefully studied the Federal Government's note of 17 November, which contains suggestions for the establishment of a four-power committee to discuss the German question. Unfortunately it is clear that the Federal Government persists in its unrealistic attitude with regard to the functions of this committee, since it again brings up the question of a discussion of the reunification of Germany by representatives of the four powers. At the same time the question of a peace treaty is pushed aside as of secondary importance, although preparations for such a treaty are a kind of first hurdle which must be cleared before any settlement of the German problem as a whole can be tackled. The latest note from the Federal Government sets out to be a kind of compromise solution whilst no attempt has been made to consider seriously the Confederation proposals by the German Democratic Republic, although under the present circumstances these represent a practical and realistic programme for the peaceful reunification of Germany. This note is typical of the Federal Government's persistent unwillingness to enter into negotiations, and shows only a desire to annex the German Democratic Republic. Once we approach the question of reunification in this manner, we must realize that the German Democratic Republic is for its part equally justified in contemplating putting to an end the system of government in the German Federal Republic. It is clear that this will not lead to a solution of the national problems facing the Germans, but merely aggravates the situation still further.

. . .

The Soviet Government, adhering to the principle of complete respect for the sovereignty of the German Democratic Republic, will, at the appropriate time, enter into negotiations with the Government of that state with a view of transferring to it certain functions temporarily carried out by the Soviet Government in pursuance of the allied agreements on Germany and Berlin, in particular the agreement between the Soviet Union and the German Democratic Republic of 20 September 1955. This would be done bearing in mind that the

German Democratic Republic, like any other independent state must have complete competence in all matters concerning its own territory, i.e., sovereignty on land, on the sea and in the air. At the same time the Soviet Government supports the plan for giving Berlin the status of a demilitarized Free City with an independent government and administration. Corresponding proposals by the Soviet Government are set out at length in the enclosed copy of the note to the Government of the United States of America.

To ensure that the steps it intends to take are not wrongly interpreted, the Soviet Government thinks it advisable to stress the following points: The Soviet Government has no intention of incorporating West Berlin into the German Democratic Republic, nor does it envisage any territorial or other gains. There can be no question of an automatic reunification of the two parts of the city, apart from anything else because on the two sides of the Brandenburg Gate two different ways of life prevail, a socialist one in East Berlin and one based on private property in the West. In other words, the Soviet Union does not suggest putting an end to the present scheme of things, but is in favour of West Berlin living as its population think best. If their choice should be for the existing social order, then it shall be according to their wish, and the Soviet Union will respect the Free City independently of its system of government and social order.

The Soviet Government is prepared, together with other states, to sign a guarantee of independence for the Free City of West Berlin. The United Nations Organization could help in ensuring that this promise was kept. In view of the insular situation of West Berlin, it would of course be necessary to come to some agreement with the German Democratic Republic about unhampered contact, for instance travel and the import and export of goods, between the Free City and the outside world in both West and East. West Berlin in its turn will have to undertake to forbid any seditious activity directed against the state in which it lies, and to accept the status of a demilitarized city. The Soviet Government solemnly promises to do its utmost to ensure normal conditions of life for the Free City as an independent economic entity. It believes it to be possible to create circumstances for the Free City in which it could enjoy a stable and full economic life. If necessary the Soviet Government is prepared to take over some of the burden from the West Berlin industry by supplying the required raw materials and foodstuffs on a commercial basis. It is the wish of the Soviet Government that the new status of West Berlin as a Free City should be to the advantage of its population, and that West Berlin should be in a position to carry on trade with whatever country suits its interests best, that industry and craftsmanship should flourish, and that conditions should be created conducive to an increase in the employment and welfare of the population. The Soviet Government, in proposing that the occupation-regime in West Berlin should be brought to an end, expects that its proposal will be carried through after six months, so that the three Western Powers and the Federal Republic can make preparations for the altered status of West Berlin and carry out the alterations smoothly. The Soviet Government considers this period completely adequate for the Governments of the United States of America, Great Britain and France to reach a sound basis for the solution of any problems that should arise. Finding a solution to the Berlin question and thus relieving international tension will be a good opportunity for both sides to show their good will in concrete action.

The Soviet Government is of the opinion that the ending of the occupation regime in Berlin will contribute much to peace and to the normalization of the German situation. It hopes that the Federal Government will appreciate the motives which have inspired it to take the steps outlined in this note and in the notes to the Governments of the United States of America, Great Britain and France.

Appendix XIV

Communiqué by the Foreign Ministers of France, the Federal Republic of Germany, the United Kingdom, and the United States, December 14, 1958

The Foreign Ministers of France, the Federal Republic of Germany, the United Kingdom and the United States met on December 14, 1958 in Paris to discuss developments in the Berlin situation during the past month, including notes addressed to their several governments on November 27 by the Soviet Union. The four Foreign Ministers had the benefit of an oral statement on the situation in Berlin by Herr Brandt, Governing Mayor of that city.

The Foreign Ministers of France, the United Kingdom and the United States once more reaffirmed the determination of their governments to maintain their position and their rights with respect to Berlin including the right of free access.

They found unacceptable a unilateral repudiation by the Soviet Government of its obligations to the Governments of France, the United Kingdom and the United States in relation to their presence in Berlin and the freedom of access to that city or the substitution of the German authorities of the Soviet Zone for the Soviet Government insofar as those rights are concerned.

After further discussion of the Soviet notes of November 27, 1958 the four Foreign Ministers found themselves in agreement on the basic issues to be dealt with in the replies to those notes. They will consult with their allies in the NATO Council, following which the four governments will formulate their replies.